The Actor Sings

D1125282

The Actor Sings

Discovering a Musical Voice for the Stage

Kevin Robison

HEINEMANN
Portsmouth, NH

Ypsilanti District Library
5577 Whittaker Rd.
Ypsilanti, MI 48197-9752

Heinemann
A division of Reed Elsevier Inc.
361 Hanover Street
Portsmouth, NH 03801–3912
www.heinemanndrama.com

Offices and agents throughout the world

© 2000 by Kevin Robison

All rights reserved. No part of this book may be reproduced in any form or by any electronic or mechanical means, including information storage and retrieval systems, without permission in writing from the publisher, except by a reviewer, who may quote brief passages in a review.

The author and publisher wish to thank those who have generously given permission to reprint borrowed material:

Figure 5–1 on page 35 illustrated by Jim Allen.

Library of Congress Cataloging-in-Publication Data
Robison, Kevin.
   The actor sings: discovering a musical voice for the stage / Kevin Robison.
      p. cm.
   Includes bibliographical references.
   ISBN 0-325-00177-4 (pbk.: acid-free paper)
     1. Musical theater—Instruction and study. 2. Singing—Instruction and study. I. Title.
MT956.R63 2000
792.6'028—dc21

                                       99-086171

Editor: Lisa A. Barnett
Production coordination: Sonja Chapman
Production service: Melissa L. Inglis
Cover design: Michael Leary Design
Manufacturing: Deanna Richardson
Back cover photo by Anne Terpstra

Printed in the United States of America on acid-free paper
04 03 02 01 00   DA   1 2 3 4 5

To Robert Allen Holder,
for cultivating my passion for theatre,
and for his eternal friendship.

Contents

Foreword

It was 1975. I was a nervous twenty-year-old. A nervous, trembling twenty-year-old music major about to take his first required voice class. My major instrument was the clarinet—I knew *nothing* about singing. Nonetheless, the class would dramatically change my life.

During my college years, I spent much time practicing and playing in various concert and musical theatre orchestras. In addition to my passion for music, I was drawn to the theatre. When I wasn't playing in the pit for musicals at San Jose State University, I could be found auditioning for nonmusical plays. In spite of my decided interest, I never really considered the possibility that I might be suited for musical theatre—especially since I'd never explored my singing voice.

My roommates at the time had told me on numerous occasions that I could not sing. We would be listening to musical theatre cast albums in our apartment and they would laugh at me every time I opened my mouth to sing along. It became a running joke among my friends that I was a great clarinet player, a good actor, but couldn't carry a tune to save my life. So when it came time to take my voice class, I was convinced I would fail. As an instrumentalist, issues of intonation and pitch are relatively easy: you create a breath, initiate some sort of external action, and the instrument speaks. But using my *voice*— no keys, no pads, no strings, just naked breath—was like learning a new instrument. Only scarier. My pitch was anywhere from a half-step to an octave off. I sounded like a bad impression of Jerry Lewis clearing his throat.

So with encouragement from my voice teacher, I not only attended class, but took private voice lessons as well. In a year's time I never once performed a song. "You're not ready," my teacher would tell me. Exercises, exercises, exercises. Throughout the term, I spent hour after hour simply trying to match pitch. This was an interesting problem for a musician. I could tell when I was playing my clarinet out of tune, I could tell when other singers were not matching pitch, but I had no idea how to do it with my own voice.

I would soon discover that matching pitch was not just a matter of *hearing* tones correctly, it was also about knowing how to physically produce them. This meant developing a sense of trust—trust in my teacher and myself. With each repetition I found more and more connections to what the process really meant. I had to *allow* my voice to be released confidently. I also had to listen to myself objectively, from *outside* the body, not just internally. Any assured, sane person would probably have given up on himself but for some reason I stuck it out—and I'm glad I did. From my perseverance came an appreciation for singing, the vocal instrument, the camaraderie of a chorus of singers, and the importance of healthy vocal technique.

At the end of my first year of study, I passed my singing final with flying colors—*in front of other people!* While no one could say I was ready for the Met, I had shown remarkable improvement and could no longer consider myself a "non-singer." I soon discovered that the joy of singing substantially outweighed my fear of it and my ability to match pitch became a non-issue. It was then that I began to pursue singing for the right reasons. It would no longer be a ritual of pass/fail exercises, but a legitimate form of expressing myself. To sing meant to be alive and to share myself in ways I never thought possible. So I shucked the reeds, Webern, and Richard Stoltzman for throat lozenges, Schumann and Richard Tucker. I came to discover many things about this newly found instrument. I had found myself—my voice.

After college, I continued vocal study with various teachers. By this point I had landed numerous small roles in theatre and spent much of my time on the road listening to recordings of my favorite singers, trying to discern exactly what it was that made them so great. I soon discovered that a singer had to have two basic skills: a moderate to advanced knowledge of vocal technique, and a profound understanding of how to communicate a song. With this discovery I was able to begin merging musician and actor into one fluid performer.

Fifteen years later I began to audition for major musicals in New York and my efforts truly began to pay off. It was 1990 and I had made the final callback for a new show from the writers of *Les Miserables*. I'll never forget landing that ensemble role. For several years I would perform in the company of *Miss Saigon* while understudying various roles in the show. It wasn't long before I found myself covering the leading role of the Engineer. By the end of the Broadway run, I was playing the part and was asked to continue with the national tour, which I've been doing ever since.

As I look back at more than twenty years of singing—the enjoyment, the hard work, the successes—I sometimes wonder what my life's path may have led to if I hadn't been sparked by that one encouraging teacher. The approach of this book reminds me much of that teacher. With clarity and honesty, Kevin Robison addresses many of the problems and fears that so many actors have shared. Of course, matching pitch and perfecting your vocal technique cannot be learned from a book, but this text will provide you with some very important tools: the knowledge that fears can be overcome, skills can be learned, and honest emotion can be shared through singing.

I wasn't a "natural" singer. In fact, my obstacles were about as profound as they could be. The truth is most of us match pitch automatically. So I believe if I could do it, anyone can. I believe, as Kevin does, that each of us has a unique voice and singing is something that *can* be learned. Sure it's hard work, but anything worth having takes an earnest effort. In this case, the payoff is indescribable.

Not only is singing a wonderful confidence-builder, it is a joyful expression of the human spirit. It's even therapeutic! My hope is that you will take to heart what is offered here and embark on the journey of discovering your voice. I know you will find success, as I and many others have. Happy singing!

—Joseph Anthony Foronda
"Engineer," *Miss Saigon*, National Tour

Acknowledgments

Believing that no one writes a book such as this by himself, I must first honor the work of authors Richard Miller, James McKinney, Kristin Linklater, and Pauline Oliveros—four people whom I've never met, yet whose influences are apparent throughout the text.

I am indebted to Patricia Troxel for encouraging me to write, for reading drafts of the manuscript at various stages, and for offering invaluable input. I'm also deeply grateful to my editor, Lisa Barnett, for her unfailing tenacity and wisdom. Without their support, this book could not have been written.

I must also acknowledge three remarkably gifted teachers, Dr. James Daugherty, Dr. Sue Snyder, and Dr. Bruce Mayhall, who set me on the path of respect for singing and taught me what it means to be a musician and teacher.

I am grateful for the help of Dr. Lynda Gantt, Ph.D., who provided invaluable insight into the psychology of singing, clarifying many concepts in the early chapters.

Sincere gratitude is also extended to Joan Melton, Judith Bettinger, Jack Greenman, and Kitty Balay, whose professional opinions about acting and singing have been instrumental in shaping the content of this book; to John Loschmann, for showing me that many technical problems in singing are resolved in the acting process; to those who've offered creative suggestions and/or shared personal experiences, including Ken Bausano, Mark Booher, Regan Carrington, Roger DeLaurier, Kimberly Emerson, Joseph Foronda, Ed Hopkins, Rebecca Judd, Carolyn Keith, Joy Scheib, and Michael Tremblay; and to Shelley Davis for her meticulous proofreading of the chapters on technique.

Finally, I must acknowledge my colleague and friend, Jeremy Mann, for remaining a constant inspiration and for convincing me that there was a great need for this book.

Introduction

"Thank you for the monologue. Do you have a song prepared?"

Have you ever had to answer "No" to this question? In New York and regional theatres across America, countless actors avoid musical auditions every day because they don't sing. In some cases, an actor won't even get in the door of a general audition without a song, much less be offered a role in a musical. And because many regional theatres cast entire seasons at once, casting directors often look for actors who can play both musical and nonmusical roles, giving those who sing a distinct advantage.

An actor doesn't have to be cast in a full-length musical to face the prospect of singing. Nearly half of Shakespeare's thirty-nine plays contain characters who sing at least one song—as do many contemporary works such as *Agnes of God, Mother Courage,* and *Lend Me a Tenor.* The actor who does not sing can seldom be considered for such roles. Combine this with the number of new musicals, revivals, and revues that appear in regional and Broadway theatres each year, and it's easy to see that singing and acting are not mutually exclusive venues.

So if the advantages of being a singer are so significant, why don't more actors learn to sing? The primary reason is that many of us do not view ourselves as singers to begin with, thereby making it extremely difficult to learn the skills. We can experience overwhelming fear and anxiety when it comes to singing. Fear of failure causes us to underestimate our own abilities or recall experiences that contribute to our anxiety. In general, we neglect developing aspects of our talent that might not live up to our own expectations. In this respect, singing remains the most neglected skill in theatre, making it the poster child for unpursued talent.

Many of us believe that in order to be great at something, we must devote one hundred percent of our energy toward it. There's something to be said for this approach, but how specific and limiting do we really want to be? By pursuing only what we do best, and pulling the "no talent" card for other skills, we perpetuate unwanted stereotypes such as "actors who (sort of) sing" or "singers who (sort of) act." I hope this book will demonstrate that singing and acting are *not* separate events. Acting cloaks itself in many forms, the least of which is singing.

"But what about talent?" you may ask. "Don't you have to have talent for singing?" Many of us believe that since a great voice was not imparted to us at birth, attempting to develop one would be futile. This is because we continue to shroud singing in mystery and intimidation, believing that very little is known about the voice and that no one can really be taught how to sing. Nothing could be further from the truth.

One reason we don't inherently know how to sing is that it's not a form of communication we use in everyday life. We don't arrive at work in the morning and greet our colleagues with musical salutations or production numbers, or find ourselves singing impassioned soliloquies when our emotions are rampant (though we may desperately want to). When we do sing, the song is usually one we already know, sung in the shower or car; a hymn sung along with a church congregation; or part of some rehearsed performance. Given this fact, there's no reason why anyone should inherently know how to walk out on stage and live truthfully in a song. As many success stories demonstrate, however, using the voice properly and communicating a song effectively are things that *can* be learned.

Modern vocal technique has been hundreds of years in the making, and with the technological advances of this century, we know more about the voice than ever before. This knowledge has opened the door for new approaches, many of which work wonders with the beginner. I have witnessed many actors make the journey from knowing nothing about singing to creating fabulous musical theatre careers for themselves. As I say to my students, a person who believes she doesn't have the talent for singing has not yet opened her mind to the process of learning the necessary skills.

Since you're reading this book, you are no doubt curious about your ability as a singer, in spite of any thoughts you may have to the contrary. I encourage you to nurture your curiosity until it grows into a burning desire. Strong determination is imperative for success in singing. Without it, a singer can easily become hypercritical, cynical, and discouraged. This book is designed to launch you into an exploration of your voice while keeping a positive outlook toward your progress. Here you will find a discussion of what it means to sing, help in overcoming anxiety, and most importantly, an explanation of how your voice works. My hope is that by the time you reach the end of the book, you will have discovered your own unique singing voice and will be ready to pursue the necessary skills with a qualified teacher.

There is a lot of information in this book, and it's important to read it sequentially. Don't read it in one sitting, attempting to do every exercise right away. This will lead to frustration that you don't need. Instead, follow the guidelines suggested below, allowing yourself ample time to process information and experiences.

Part I of this book addresses many issues and obstacles that typically stand in the path of the actor who has not yet found a singing voice. Some of the issues may not apply to you, but don't ignore them—they are essential to understanding the process of singing. Allow yourself several days to read and ponder these early chapters before moving on.

Part II allows you to make important connections between speaking and singing and also contains an overview of how your voice works. In addition, it offers simple exercises for acquiring the necessary skills for singing. Information found here will likely be reiterated and expounded upon by a qualified teacher. Allow yourself to experience each chapter for several days before moving on.

Part III offers practical advice on finding a teacher, performing a song, and preparing for your first musical audition. These chapters will serve as important references on the journey of discovering your singing voice.

On a personal note, I have tremendous passion for this subject—passion that I hope will transcend these pages and enable you to take bold steps forward with commitment and enthusiasm. Singing is a passionate experience, enabling us to communicate on a much higher plane than we do in everyday life. It is also a healing experience, one that liberates the mind, body, and soul. Singing is therefore an essential art, one that we all want and need to experience—it's simply part of our human existence.

So if you're a human being with a voice to say the words "I am a singer, I am entitled to sing," then you have the tools you need to begin your journey. What's exciting is that your voice is unique, unlike any other, offering you a singular perspective and advantage. So proceed with an open mind and spirit, and be prepared to change your mind about what you're capable of. It is only in the process of exploration that important discoveries are made.

I

Revealing a Singing Actor

"Singing is too important to be left to the singers."

—Unknown

• • • 1 •So Many Possibilities . . .

I learned to sing as a youth in a fundamental church environment in the South. I had no training whatsoever beyond that of
listening to gospel albums and to a few people I heard at my
church. Looking back, the quality of sound that I produced was
very nasal and had precious little to offer in the way of resonance
or stability; I was very young and knew nothing beyond my
everyday singing voice.

When I joined the high school choir, I had to learn to sing in
a completely different manner. I acquired the skills for proper
breathing, modification of vowels, and expanded resonance, all
of which were required for ensemble singing. My voice changed
dramatically in just one year, and I went from singing gospel in
church to receiving recognition in regional high school competitions and statewide events. I allowed my voice to be transformed.

But when I decided to major in voice in college, I discovered that my work had only just begun. My teacher tried dili-
gently to get me to open up the sound and allow it to resonate
with a freely produced vibrato. We spent a full year in my under-
graduate program struggling with the fact that I was "holding"
my voice in place and not releasing it freely. The more we tried,
the more frustrated I became. One day, as my teacher was
patiently coaching me through the process, I just blurted out the
most pretentious operatic voice I could muster, singing my
Italian art song as though I were Pavarotti himself. Before I was
even through the first phrase, my teacher jumped up from the
piano bench and started shouting at me. At first I thought she
was angry, but then I realized that she was shouting, "Yes! Yes,
Kevin! That's it!" Startled and confused, I retorted, "No, no,
that's *not* it, because that's not *me*!"

A few awkward moments passed and then she finally said,
"Well, if it wasn't you, then who was it?" Of course I had no

reply to this, she was exactly right: *I* had made that sound, no one else.

This bold choice represented a departure from the norm for me and a turning point in my study. I learned that if I wanted to sing opera, I had to release my voice and be willing to *sound* like an opera singer. I discovered that no amount of work on my teacher's part was going to do it for me as long as I resisted. My eyes and ears were opened to the idea of creating a new vocabulary of sounds for my voice. Once again, I allowed it to be transformed.

In allowing my voice to take on shapes and styles that were not part of my everyday speaking and singing voice, I discovered a world of performance options, from pop to musical theatre to opera. I explored the characteristics of particular styles and was able to apply my voice in a healthy manner to most any style.

Developing characteristics of a style must not be confused with imitating a particular singer, however. The fact is that no two voices are alike, and the singer who attempts to replicate the sound of another is only going to succeed at imitation. In addition, he is in danger of robbing himself of the natural beauty of his own voice and jeopardizing his vocal health. A singer must be willing to accept the inherent natural beauty of his own voice in order to release it freely and honestly. Like acting, singing must be done with complete honesty and a willingness for self-discovery. Any attempts at manufacturing a voice will invariably lead to self-betrayal.

For each of us, there exists a continuum of vocal styles, enabling us to produce a variety of sounds. Since theatre roles exist at most every point, we must be willing to experience as many styles as possible. It's amazing how quickly we can put the results of such exploration to work, too. Unlike opera, it's not necessary to wait until years of vocal training have amassed before singing for the first time. There are singing roles for anyone in the theatre who can match pitch, activate a lyric, and be comfortable with her voice; but for an actor to determine what roles are appropriate for her, a significant amount of exploration must happen.

Exploring the voice means going beyond what is considered the norm. For most of us, the norm is what I call the "shower and car voice." This voice is the one we use when no one else is listening and represents our most natural, uninhibited state. It serves the purpose of singing along with the radio or tape player in our cars, and while it may be lovely, it's most likely underdeveloped. Many people who claim they can't sing have based their total vocal potential on the sound of this untrained voice. They assume it is all they will ever know.

As actors, we are constantly transforming our voices and bodies to accommodate a variety of characters. This means we must learn to speak and move in a variety of ways different from our everyday demeanor. Using our ordinary speaking voice when performing Shakespeare, for example, is generally unacceptable— we must expand our vocal size to match the parlance of his style; the same is true for Shaw, Brecht, or any other playwright who uses language in a heightened manner. Singing requires us to do the same: we must be willing to expand and transform the voice into a shape that may not reflect our individual persona.

So, if you consider yourself a strong actor, then you must consider the possibility that you're a strong singer, regardless of what you may think about your present vocal quality. The process of exploring your voice may lead to some surprising results. The more you sing, the more comfortable you'll become living in the world of your voice and adapting to its environment. It's like visiting a foreign country—if you go there often enough, you learn to speak the language and to function in the surroundings. Once you live in the surroundings, you can modify and improve them at will.

There is an enormous need for balance between acting and singing skills in the theatre. While revealing a useful singing voice is not that difficult, developing one that can compete in today's business is a distinct challenge. We can hope for the day when we all can act and sing equally well, but we must first demand it of ourselves.

What It Means to Sing

While it's not absolutely necessary for every actor to sing, every singer must be able to act. Good acting depends on trust—trusting oneself and an acting partner to give and take what is needed in a given moment. By trusting, an actor becomes vulnerable, enabling himself to be affected and changed by the actions of another. In doing so, he is able to deliver a performance that is truthful, present, and spontaneous.

The same is true for singing. A singer who doesn't act a song doesn't communicate the lyric and therefore doesn't really sing it. Like acting, singing requires us to be *present* in the current moment. This is difficult because singing requires us to adhere to particular notes and rhythms, which limits our spontaneity. Nonetheless, truthful communication must be a priority in singing, especially if one considers himself an actor.

For years, opera singers have been forgiven their shortcomings as actors in light of their superior voices. Today, as more and more singers discover the importance of studying acting, operatic performances are improving significantly. In fact, many singers find that the only time their vocal technique truly serves them is when they connect emotionally—that is, when they act.

While it might make sense that acting is not the primary focus of opera, it's alarming to see how neglected it can be in musical theatre. Many performers seem to lay acting aside when they sing, furthering the idea that the two are somehow mutually exclusive. This is ironic, since singing represents only a portion of the performance of a role, while acting encompasses the entirety of it.

We must acknowledge, then, that *singing is a form of acting*. Perhaps it's not unreasonable to say that a song well acted is better than a song well sung. This is particularly true in contemporary musical theatre, where many roles demand more of us as actors than as singers.

The type of actor/singer required for a particular character is addressed by directors, musical directors, and producers on an individual basis. The nature of the character and the given circumstances help determine what type of voice is needed for a particular role. The vocal quality required to play Mrs. Lovett in *Sweeney Todd*, for example, is decidedly different than that of Sarah in *Ragtime*. Typically, a raw, unrefined voice is used to reflect the quirkiness of Mrs. Lovett's character, while a dramatic soprano is required to support the high stakes of Sarah's life-threatening circumstances. While an untrained singer may not be able to sustain the demands of Sarah's character, it's quite possible for a relatively inexperienced singer with strong acting ability to deliver a convincing performance of Mrs. Lovett.

The role of Billy Bigelow in *Carousel* is another that raises the issue of vocal quality in the casting process. This character is extremely unrefined, unable to hold down a job and prone to extreme physical violence, yet he has some of the most beautiful and challenging music in the show. This works because Billy's good side surfaces whenever he sings, helping to make him the sympathetic character he needs to be. But the task of reconciling beautiful music with a heated temperament leads to many questions about how the character should be cast.

The role was written for John Raitt, a trained singer with moderate acting ability, during a time when musicals were presented as much lighter fare than they are today. However, many modern productions tend to seek out the darker side of shows like *Carousel* in an attempt to create more powerful, realistic performances. In this spirit, the producers of the '94 Broadway revival chose Michael Hayden, an actor capable of reflecting Billy's insurgent nature in his singing. This led to a somewhat "less legitimate" vocal quality and brought about some criticism of Hayden's portrayal. While arguments can be made against an approach like this, most are founded in tradition and aesthetics. The fact is that audiences have come to expect Billy to sing extremely well over the years. And although a strong singer can create some lovely musical moments for him, a strong actor is required to fully realize the complexities of his character.

Some roles, if to be performed as written, should never be attempted by untrained singers, mainly for reasons of vocal stamina and health. Nonetheless, a number of performers have achieved remarkable success in musical theatre with unremarkable singing technique. How many times have we praised the work of Yul Brynner, Elaine Stritch, Nathan Lane, Natasha Richardson, and countless others who on their vocal merit alone were only average singers at best? These performers have been successful because of their ability to communicate a lyric so effectively that their vocal quality becomes of secondary importance. Listen to Carol Channing's rousing performance of "Before the Parade Passes By" (*Hello, Dolly!*), Gene Barry's earthy "Song on the Sand" (*La Cage aux Folles*), or Judi Dench's definitive "Send in the Clowns" (*A Little Night Music*, featured in *Hey, Mr. Producer! The Musical World of Cameron Mackintosh*). We grow to love these voices for their genuine, expressive qualities, not for their beauty of tone.

It's been said that singing is simply a matter of acting on pitch. While this may help put the process of singing into a workable perspective for many actors, that is not all there is to it. Healthy, productive singing requires practical application of vocal technique over an extended period of time. Nonetheless, many nonsinging actors are able to find their way into singing through the acting process with which they are familiar. Given the fact that singing is a form of acting, such an approach is logical and often useful in finding a voice.

The process of acting a song presents its own unique set of challenges. Since most of us don't experience spontaneous singing in everyday life, we are left with little in the way of personal experience from which to draw while on stage. Even if we find ourselves singing a lyric about mundane, everyday things, the process through which we communicate is more artistic than realistic. Let's face it: musical theatre by definition should not work. The suspension of disbelief it demands of an audience is huge. There's no reason we should believe that characters in a play would suddenly burst into song to express themselves. What's more, we must also believe that the singing would happen amidst lavish choreography and full orchestral accompaniment. But when a performer is effectively communicating a song and living truthfully in the moment, we find it thrilling to suspend our disbelief and go along for the ride. A strong actor, for his own sense of truth and reality, is required to make this happen.

"So where do I start?" you may ask. Well, beginning to discover your singing voice is just that: a discovery. You must be willing to explore, risk, evaluate, and build upon what you already know. It is not always easy, but the rewards are exhilarating. The first step is to know where you are now and where you would like to be. As Stephen Sondheim writes, "If you can know where you're going, you've gone."

▪ ▪ ▪ 2 ▪ Suspending Your Disbelief

There are many potential obstacles for the actor who is first learning to sing. Among them are the obvious technical challenges of aligning the body, learning to breathe, and developing a resonant sound. Of all the obstacles, however, the most common is not a technical one at all—it's the singer himself. If you have fears or doubts about your singing ability, read this chapter carefully.

Every day I encounter people whose greatest challenge with singing is to get out of their own way. For some reason they believe that singing is not in the realm of possibility. There are many complexities in the psychology of singing that overlap and intertwine, depending on the individual. In hopes that the reader can relate to some of these, I will outline a few of the more common issues. First a bit of armchair psychology, then we'll get to the singing.

Three Unfortunate Events

"Lisa"

Lisa, a former student of the conservatory where I teach, was the daughter of a man with a beautiful singing voice. He sang in church and performed in community theatre on a regular basis; everyone loved to hear him sing. At an early age, Lisa noticed how much joy he derived from singing and began to explore her own singing voice.

One day, she was in her room singing along with a record when her father walked by and quipped, "Well, you sure didn't get any of your dad's talent, did ya?" While he meant no conscious harm in this, his words struck her with brutal force and extinguished her desire to sing. For years to come, she would believe she had no singing ability at all, much less any of the talent her father had.

When she entered our conservatory program in her early twenties, she had many psychological hurdles to jump before opening her mouth to make a musical sound. She had to revisit that childhood event, put it into perspective, and learn to think differently about her singing ability. In the process, she discovered a marvelous instrument that had been dormant for years.

While Lisa hasn't forgotten that unfortunate event, she has learned to be more objective and trust her own ability. Now she performs professionally in musicals and makes her living as a singing actor.

"ALAN"

A colleague of mine, Alan, was musically inclined in his childhood and wanted desperately to become a singer. However, a speech impediment made him very self-conscious and reluctant to speak, much less sing.

When an opportunity came to join the school band, he was told he had talent for playing the trumpet. Since he felt he could never succeed as a singer, he pursued this instrument vigorously, determined to find some sort of voice in music. In his mind, the trumpet was "sent" to replace his singing voice. Although he overcame his speech impediment during his teens, Alan's fear of singing remained with him for a long time after. At some deep level, he not only felt physically deformed, he believed he was vocally inneffectual.

In his adult life, he formed a very successful swing band that featured a talented jazz vocalist. One day, an emergency situation forced the singer to miss a concert, and Alan was the only person in the group who knew the lyrics and melodies well enough to cover. While he had become moderately comfortable with his singing, he had never sung in public before.

Suddenly his childhood fear began to wreak havoc with his emotions. He remembered being teased about his speech impediment in his childhood and how the prospect of singing terrified him. The frenzied pace of the situation didn't allow him time to give in, however. Alan had no choice but to cover for the missing singer.

After the concert, he received raves about his singing, not only from fellow musicians and friends but from people he had never even met. While Alan hadn't overcome his childhood inhibitions completely, this event gave him tremendous power over them and the courage to finally consider himself a singer.

"THERESE"

Therese grew up in a traditional Methodist church environment, singing hymns and performing in the children's choir. She had a lovely singing voice that showed great promise. During one of her high school years, her choir director called on her to sing the solo in a spiritual piece. He assumed that because Therese was African American, she would automatically have the southern gospel quality called for by the solo.

When he discovered that she had no experience in this style of music, he discouraged her from singing altogether. He warned her that people would expect her to be able to sing gospel and would be disappointed when she couldn't. In spite of the fact that her mother was a noted singer trained in opera, Therese believed what her teacher had said. Had she discussed this event with her mother, she might have received the encouragement she needed and put things into perspective. Instead, she clammed up, quit the choir and stopped singing altogether.

Needless to say, Therese entered our training program with the idea that something was wrong with her singing voice. But the only thing wrong with her voice was the fact that she wasn't willing to release it. After much discussion and exploration, she has found a strong and versatile instrument waiting to be developed.

These are just a few examples of the kind of messages we receive in early life about our singing—messages that we can carry for a lifetime. Some people are told by elementary teachers that they have no singing ability; others have college professors who steer them away from musical theatre, suggesting it isn't their forte.

Some people even convince themselves they cannot sing, such as my colleague who insists that since she will never be able to sing like the great Maria Callas, she doesn't bother. In nearly every case, there is some precipitating event that reduces self-esteem and sets these beliefs into motion.

Unfortunate events like these can be overcome once we begin to embrace and release our fears. It's only when we are able to look objectively at our natural ability that we are able to discover a singing voice.

The "F" Word

Letting go of fears is easier said than done. Our impatient and competitive nature as artists makes us prone to create excuses for inadequacies, especially where learning a new skill is concerned. Many of us fabricate a sense of false modesty by making fun of ourselves with statements like "Oh, you don't want to hear *me* screeching out the notes," or "I'm as tone deaf as that chair," or even "I know that when God decides to really punish me, I'm going to have to sing in public." Some people actually become ill when they have to sing in front of others. In any case, the responses we create, whether witty or dramatic, are most often the result of fear and a distorted belief system that we have incorporated as a part of our self-image.

Most of us are principally afraid of failure. We've all heard the expression "There can be no possibility for success without the potential of failure." But the connotations of *failure* are laden with unworthiness. Everyone would benefit greatly by removing words like this from their vocabularies.

So how about: "There can be no possibility for success without room for *improvement*"? To illustrate, let's say a potter makes a pot. He declares, "This is a pot that I have made." In this simple statement, he has validated his work without commenting on the quality of it. Upon closer examination, however, he may discover some potential areas of improvement. Rather than say, "What I should have done here was this," he can choose to say, "Next time, I will improve by doing that." Rather than wallowing in failure, he offers himself a constructive critique that leads to improvement.

There is no opportunity for improvement, however, when one continues to avoid what is feared the most. Fear is a clear indication of passionate interest in a matter. If you have fears about singing, you must examine them carefully and embrace them as something positive.

Fear is the very reason we choose to not cultivate our own spiritual size or accept our inherent qualities as true and valid. If we do not first recognize our abilities as singers, we cannot begin to study vocal technique. Since the issue is a psychological one, so must be the solution. First, a change of mind and heart must occur and doing this takes courageous objectivity and a willingness to dispell our fears.

Somewhere along the way we've all learned to doubt our ability for a particular subject or skill. This is usually because someone we trust has told us we have no ability. Like the examples at the beginning of this chapter, most instances occur when we're young and impressionable. But one thing must be made clear: singing is a right, not a privilege held by the talented elite. No one should ever be told he or she cannot sing. Those who have must understand that somewhere along the way a tiny parcel of misinformation has been allowed to fester and grow into a belief.

There is no way we can expect to succeed in theatre if we take passing comments from others so seriously. Opinions held by directors, musical directors, and critics determine the "value" of our performances every day. Because of this, we must work hard to remain objective and not allow our own self-worth to be derailed. A former professor of mine describes a critic as one who sits on a hill watching a bloody battle and, upon its conclusion, runs down and kills all the survivors. It's crucial to remember that a comment made by someone else is simply a comment, neither good nor bad—what's important is how we respond to it.

We must reframe the way we receive feedback and develop alternative ways of seeing what is happening. Doing this means we must recognize self-critical thinking, assess what emotions these thoughts trigger, and change our thoughts by reframing them into positive self-statements.

In addition to guarding against destructive information, we must be willing to welcome positive feedback from respectable sources. In an interview during the run of David Hare's Broadway play *Amy's View*, actress Judi Dench was asked to explain her unique ability to connect with an audience. Her response: "Well, I'm not sure what that is, really, but David Hare tells me I'm doing it, and I believe anything that man says."

Of course it requires a great deal of courage and objectivity to know the difference between valid and invalid comments. Even so, no amount of positive messages is going to help as long as we continue to hold on to negative ones from years past. Ideally, positive messages replace negative ones, enabling us to move forward with confidence.

Whatever the issues may be for you, the first step is to name the obstacle, then work toward transforming it. Determine if there's a fear of success or failure with singing, or if there is some issue that perpetuates the belief that you have no talent. A simple understanding of where your reluctance comes from is the first step to ridding yourself of the problem. You can then effectively deal with your own resistance.

You must be willing to suspend your own disbelief and embark on the journey of singing with an open mind and spirit. Whatever tools you use to transform your fear or doubt about singing are good ones. Once these issues begin to evaporate, the process of learning the necessary skills can begin.

...3 ▪ Getting to Know You

Being able to share yourself freely is the very foundation of singing well. While it's necessary to lay aside your doubts and fears, you must also make yourself emotionally available to the process. Let's take a look at how singing, like acting, is dynamically connected to our emotions.

As newborn babies, we babble, coo, and use our voices freely. Every sound we make is musical in its own right. We allow our emotional state to govern the sounds we make. But something is lost as we get older; we become more inhibited, more self-conscious and less willing to share our voices naturally—the song we are born with is forgotten. Some of us are fortunate enough to "remember" it as we get older, but many of us are not. Aspects of our personality and emotional makeup often inhibit our ability to respond to the need for singing in our adult lives.

The inherent emotional nature of singing requires us to experience and share sensations of joy, love, or anger in an honest manner, much as we did as children. There is no such thing as apathetic singing. On top of that, the instrument through which we communicate is the human body itself, weaving the act of singing into our very being. So, before we sing a song, we must be comfortable sharing our emotional and physical bodies.

Think of singing as an extension of speaking, as though it were a normal occurrence in everyday life. First, there is an instantaneous reactionary moment to some sort of outside information or event. This is followed by a cognitive response that passes through a free and natural voice, resulting in truthful communication through song. When viewed in this way, it becomes clear that the singer who is not willing to both experience and physicalize an emotion cannot produce an emotionally convincing sound. In this sense, singing and acting are exactly the same thing.

For the actor, emotion is an available tool, accessible in the moment of creation; it is not necessarily personal. Many actors fear that because singing is such an emotional activity, they will *become* emotional in the process and lose composure. But the performer who makes himself emotionally available throughout the *process* of singing learns to manage his emotions in performance. The actor who always holds back has less emotional experience to bring to the stage. Emotion is what makes the human connection.

In a class that I was coaching recently, a student was singing a song about the pain of unrequited love. He was singing beautifully, but he wasn't connecting to the meaning of the text and therefore was not communicating it. No one could find technical fault with his singing, it's just that it wasn't engaging. This probably had to do with the fact that he was a trained musician who had been taught to focus primarily on making beautiful sounds.

The assignment for this particular class was to find a personal connection to the lyric, so I asked him if he'd be willing to tell us whom he was singing to and under what specific circumstances. He agreed and shared part of his personal story with the class. When he was finished, I asked him to let us "see" the person to whom he was singing, and to tell that person exactly how he felt.

He went back and sang the song again. As he progressed through it, his connection to the lyric became stronger. He was hardly able to finish it for the tears in his eyes. In this one exercise he had made himself emotionally available to the text for the first time. He also moved his classmates to tears. In a short while, he was able to live truthfully in his song without losing composure, and his vocal quality became even more beautiful because his singing came from an emotional place, not a technical one. He learned to trust himself and his audience.

In the days when I accompanied voice lessons for various teachers, there were instances in which a student would arrive for a lesson saying she could not sing because of an emotional crisis in her life. One teacher would typically dismiss the student who said this and tell her to come back when she had worked things out. After all, very little work could be done on vocal technique if the student were going to burst into tears. Another teacher would spend the hour trying to counsel the student, hoping that the problem could be worked out and they could eventually get to the singing. Neither of these approaches were particularly helpful, however. The first ignored the problem, the second turned the voice teacher into a therapist.

The most effective teacher in this situation was the one who embraced the problem and encouraged the student to sing through it anyway. This was often challenging, since emotions would completely overcome the singing at times. But by singing while in an emotional state, many students became more connected with an inner self, leading them to share and express themselves more freely and honestly. Once the emotion was released, the technique was supported.

A common reason for being emotionally unavailable is a preoccupation with vocal technique. While developing technique requires us to put acting aside from time to time, it can never be given up completely. Even in high opera, a beautiful tone is simply a beautiful tone. It's only when the lyric is activated by awakening emotions within the singer that anyone listening can be affected by the performance. As Helen Mirren stated, "Very technically informed intution is fantastic. . . . Really old . . . actors are brilliant because they've finally reached the point when they can let go of all technique."

Not only does emotional restraint lead to poor communication, it can also create unwanted tension in the voice, rendering performers incapable of producing beautiful sounds. Many people do not realize that their inherent emotional state controls many technical aspects of the voice: anger or criticism leads to unwanted tension in the tongue or jaw, fear and anxiety leads to sounds that are not supported, and so forth. Whenever the voice is released and allowed to resonate freely, it is inherently beautiful. When it is controlled in any conscious or subconscious way, it suffers.

Think for a moment how your emotions are directly connected to your voice: Whenever you are happy, you *sound* happy; when you're angry, it's indicated in your tone. Harbored feelings can interfere with healthy vocal production as well. For example, it's possible for residual anger to create tension in the jaw, even if the singer doesn't feel angry when he sings. Each of us is unique, as is the way we physically respond to our emotions. In first learning to sing, you must get to know yourself completely: how you learn, what motivates and inspires you, and what you really desire to achieve. You must like yourself.

Learning the proper skills for singing is dependent upon releasing your fear, your doubt, and your emotional self. Understand that doing this is a process, not a single action. You will spend the rest of your life exploring how certain elements of technique work for you, but if you're not willing to explore the emotional tools—optimism, desire, determination, vulnerability, objectivity, and an overall passion for learning more about yourself—the physical tools will simply not work.

As an actor, you can see the inherent benefits of exploring your singing voice, even if you don't actually put the knowledge to practical application. It's an actor's job to know as much about herself as possible. Singing is a great path to this self-discovery because it can teach you a great deal about who you are. This is without a doubt the most important reason to pursue your singing voice.

....4 .I Can Do That!

Once upon a time there were two brothers: See and Saw. Both had a strong interest in building toys and spent much of their time making wooden amusements for the children in their neighborhood. See, however, was apparently more talented than Saw. Everyone noticed right away that he was more creative and paid closer attention to detail. Saw's toys showed definite promise and practicality, but they just weren't as colorful or as interesting.

After a while, Saw noticed something about his brother's work: it wasn't durable. See's toys were breaking after a short period of time and the children were throwing them away. Saw had an idea: "What if I can build something that's not only creative but also lasting?" He set out to find the information he needed by observing the carpenters in their town and asking them all sorts of questions. He also read everything he could find relating to the subject of making toys.

After several years of experimenting and learning, Saw began to build toys again. By this time, he was confident in the durability of his work and was able to focus on being more creative. See, on the other hand, continued to rely on his natural talent and, while he continued to build toys for many years, they were never as popular or as durable as his brother's.

This simple story illustrates an important point: There is a significant difference between talent and skill. A skill is an ability, an expertise or proficiency. It's something that one does well and is acquired through means of study or hands-on experience. Many carpenters, for example, learn to build structures by observing or working alongside more experienced craftsmen. Through a process of mentoring, a carpenter develops skills that enable him to design and create his own product.

Yet there are times when a person with a penchant for building seems to naturally know how to do things. For some reason he is able to design and build his own structure without the aid of a teacher. Perhaps he only needs to learn how the tools work or simply observe the finished product of another in order to build his own product right away. This person is not only skillful, he is talented.

Having talent means possessing a set of specialized skills that one has seemingly not studied or learned from anyone else. An entire book could be written speculating why some people have particular talents and others do not. Even those who possess natural ability often cannot account for it.

It makes sense that the performer who understands what she does and why she does it has an advantage over the one who relies on natural ability she doesn't really understand. By studying the "whats" and "whys" of a particular technique, a performer can incorporate new skills into her existing talent. Many successful singers start with average voices and achieve great notoriety by developing the necessary skills. So rather than viewing singing as a mysterious talent, you must consider it a set of skills that are not yet developed.

Beginning to learn a new skill can be formidable at first—especially as we get older. The process of singing requires a healthy dose of patience while the muscles of the vocal mechanism are being trained to respond in new ways. Of course the success of anyone who studies singing will vary. The discovery process yields a variety of vocal options, from spirited character to romantic lead. There are many different roles to be played: Some characters need to sing well, others do not, and with such a wide range of options, there are singing roles for everyone.

The Essentials

Because we've used our voices and bodies every day since infancy, we have all developed physicalities that are uniquely ours. Unfortunately, we're not given an instruction manual that tells us how to use our body—we simply do with it the best we can.

When we begin to study acting, singing, or dance, we discover certain physicalities that prove to inhibit the performing process must be given up and replaced with useful ones. The saying "Old habits die hard" is not just cliche, it's absolute truth.

Understanding what types of habits you already possess will help you in creating necessary ones for successful singing. While many habits have to do with issues of breath management, physical alignment, and vocal placement (described in later chapters), the most important ones to develop are those of matching pitch and rhythm. I call these skills "habits" because once they're mastered, they serve us automatically without conscious thought in performance.

To be a successful singer, one must demonstrate the ability to sing specific pitches (notes) and rhythms (patterns in time) as written by the composer. Matching pitch and rhythm is dependent upon one's ability to process outside information and respond to it in a consistent manner.

When we hear a pitch, the auditory nerve inside our ear sends an electronic message to our brain, which forwards it to our vocal mechanism, enabling us to replicate the sound. Unless there is some sort of physical problem with the auditory nerve, the proper message is always sent, making it impossible for anyone with normal hearing to be "tone deaf."

How our body responds to this message can vary, however. It's possible for information being transmitted to the brain to be misinterpreted (just as we misunderstand communication from others), causing a singer to produce a different pitch. Here's why: Not only does the auditory nerve hear a primary pitch that is played or sung, it hears *overtones* of that pitch as well. Overtones are other pitches that are related to the primary pitch but are less prominent to the ear. For most of us, the brain naturally filters out overtones and focuses on the primary sound. If our brain has not been trained to do this, we are likely to sing the wrong note.

For many people, matching the sound of another same-sex voice is easier than matching a tone produced on the piano or some other instrument. When the auditory nerve transmits the sound of another voice in the same range, the brain has less "interpreting" to do. This means the singer is more likely to correctly match the pitch.

Developing a sense of rhythm is a bit more precarious. Fortunately, it's less frequently a problem. Considering the fact that our heart beats at a fairly consistent rate, rhythm is inherent in our bodies . We display a sense of rhythm in many everyday activities as well, such as running, walking and applauding, all of which happen at a (reasonably) steady pace. Keeping time in music and internalizing the rhythm of a song is a much more natural process than it would seem.

For many, the ability to match pitch and rhythm comes naturally, but for some of us, one or both of these skills is not yet developed. Sometimes we're labeled "tone deaf" or as "having no sense of rhythm." But this can be the case only if there is a fundamental problem with the auditory nerve, a very rare condition. The way in which one goes about developing the ability to match pitch is not universal; it varies from one person to the next. For those with serious pitch issues, a mentor is required to monitor the learning process and to help the singer hear the difference between correct and incorrect responses. This can only be done through patient repetition and a willingness to remain objective. Among those with normal hearing and a strong sense of determination, I have seen a success rate of one hundred percent.

A friend of mine auditioned for her theatre department's production of a musical when she was a freshman in college. She was in every way right for a particular part, except that she had severe pitch problems when she sang. Proving to be the best person available for the role, however, she was cast. She struggled with her character's song throughout the rehearsal process but to no avail. In a valiant effort to keep her on pitch, the director and musical director finally agreed upon a workable solution and turned the number into a duet. Having someone else sing with her was the only way to keep her on pitch. She was quite discouraged by the situation but didn't allow herself to be convinced she couldn't sing.

Having survived a very difficult run, she began to take voice lessons, determined that this would not happen to her again. She found an excellent voice teacher in the college music department who helped her with vocal development and ear training. In four years she had completed a degree in theatre with a minor in music, singing solos in concerts and performing with a professional opera company. Shortly thereafter she moved to New York and soon landed roles in Broadway productions of *The Secret Garden*, *Sweeney Todd*, and *Phantom of the Opera*. For her, developing the habits of matching pitch and rhythm led to the discovery of a fabulous singing instrument.

Don't assume that matching pitch or rhythm will be a challenge for you just because there's been a discussion of the subject here. Remember that each person and each voice is unique; we all approach singing from different emotional and physical places and face unique challenges. Most voice teachers will expect you to be able to manage pitch and rhythm issues before beginning your study. If you feel either is a problem for you, be up-front with a potential teacher and ask about his or her willingness to work with you on these skills. Once they are in place, you can begin to learn actual technique.

The Singer's DNA

Throughout the process of crafting our performing skills, we hear the word *technique* quite often—perhaps too often. Technique is the way in which a person uses his voice, body, and mind to coordinate the process of performing. It is built by training the body and mind to respond to certain impulses in specific ways. As actors, singers, and dancers, we spend years developing technical proficiency in areas of diction, dialect, physical movement, and muscular development. While building strong technique is essential to improving our skills, it cannot be an active part of performing. Technique is something that must be perfected in a studio and left there.

In singing, good technique should be both physical and mental, coordinating the mind and body in particular ways to achieve an aesthetic product. While opinions about technique vary and are highly subjective, it is generally referred to as "good" when a performer achieves the most with the least investment. One must work hard to achieve solid technique, which in turn makes performing as effortless as possible.

Actor Hume Cronyn once referred to technique as "[the] means by which the actor can get the best out of himself. It's as simple and as broad as that—and as personal and private." This is also true for singing: no two singers produce the same sound the same way. But having a basic knowledge of how the voice works enables a singer to make sounds that are known to be healthy and free.

Dependable principles must be employed to prevent the voice from becoming ill or damaged. Just because a particular sound may feel right doesn't mean it's healthy. Good technique produces healthy singing, and healthy singing produces consistency and reliability in performance. The goal of studying vocal technique is to always know what will happen in performance, eliminating any questions about how your voice will serve you on stage.

Part II of this book outlines the basic physical tools needed for singing: understanding that singing is an extension of speech, managing the breath, developing an awareness of your vocal apparatus, experiencing sensations of resonance, and an overview of your articulators. This information is derived from several well-known methods of beginning technique and is the necessary foundation for any type of singing, from pop music to musical theatre to opera. Some ideas are hundreds of years old, others are the result of modern thinking and scientific study. The more basic the concept, the more widely accepted it tends to be. The further one delves into technique, the more complex the concepts become.

In the chapters that follow I offer a concise introduction with terminology chosen specifically for the actor. You will embark on a sometimes technical, sometimes image-based journey into the singing voice. Proceed with caution, however: *what follows is not meant as a substitute for studying voice with a qualified teacher.* The voice is a delicate instrument designed to serve you in both speech and song and can be damaged over time if not monitored properly.

Different teachers approach technique in different ways, so terminology may vary once you enter a studio with this information. Even when one studies a prescribed technique from beginning to end, she must make adjustments and concessions that work uniquely for her. Developing one's technique is an ongoing process—one that is enigmatic at best. It's the performer's DNA.

II

Releasing Your Voice

*"Inspiration cannot be commanded, it is capricious.
That is why the actor must always have
a strong technique to fall back on."*

—Michael Chekhov

. . . 5 . From Speaking to Singing

As stated earlier, singing is not a natural daily occurrence, but it is a natural function of the voice. It is, in effect, a heightened form of speaking. The same synapses and muscles are used in both speaking and singing, just in slightly different ways. What follows is a simple description of the technical process from the inception of a sound through its release:

- The origin of any spoken or sung sound is an impulse that occurs in the brain. This impulse is timed to arrive at various areas of the body that are coordinated to produce some sort of vocal sound.

- The first muscle to receive this impulse is the diaphragm. The diaphragm is a horizontal muscle connected to the bottom of the lungs, lying between the rib cage and the stomach area (see figure 5–1 on page 35). Its natural position is an upward curve that contracts downward upon receiving an impulse. As it moves down, the lungs are stretched and the mouth, larynx, and esophagus are opened, causing outside air to rush into the lungs.

- The lungs inflate with air, and, with the help of other muscles, cause the rib cage to expand. Once enough breath has been amassed for the desired sound, it is redirected outward, causing the diaphragm to relax upward to its natural position.

- As breath is released, it meets with resistance from the vocal folds, or vocal cords, in the larynx (the voice box in the front part of the neck). The vibrating vocal folds transfer the breath into sound.

- This energized sound creates secondary vibrations in the chest and neck that amplify the sound. Vibrations in the

29

vocal folds are transferred onto the breath, which carries the sound into the head, where the sinuses, soft palate, and other chambers amplify the sound further.

- The lips, tongue, and jaw muscles are then coordinated to mold the general sound into a specific sound or word and together provide an articulatory system for the voice.

The process by which spoken and sung sounds are produced is essentially the same, except that singing requires a greater impulse. With a greater impulse comes more breath capacity, stronger vibrations in the vocal folds, and increased resonance in the overall sound.

The following exercises will help illustrate this point. Remember that singing is a process, and exercises contribute to that process. As you follow the suggestions in this and subsequent chapters, guard against the tendency to judge your efforts as "right" or "wrong." Allow the process to develop naturally. Each time you perform an exercise, you will learn something that will make it more useful to you.

Exploring Your Speaking Voice

You should be in a room alone, sitting comfortably in a chair, completely relaxed and uninhibited. Take a moment and read this paragraph out loud. Notice the *quality* of sound in your speaking voice. Note that the quality of your voice is simply what makes it your own; it doesn't judge your voice as sounding good or bad. Continue reading out loud and gradually raise the intensity of your voice. This might be the area of your voice you would use if you were reading to a large group of people or if you were on stage in performance. Notice how much more breath it takes to use this part of your voice.

Now read this section out loud and move back and forth from the normal speaking voice to the more present stage voice. You'll notice there's a conversational area, where you would speak if you were sitting next to a friend; an elevated area, where you might speak to a friend across the room; and a declamatory area, where you might speak to a room full of people.

The latter sound you produced is very much like singing, the difference being that singing requires sustaining each sound on a designated pitch.

A pitch is the location of a musical sound on a scale from low to high and is determined by the frequency of vibrations in the sound. Where the human voice has vocal folds, for example, pianos, guitars, and violins have strings that enable us to play certain pitches by altering the frequency of their vibrations.

The Musicality of Your Speaking Voice

Ask the following question out loud: "Could you direct me to the post office?" Notice how the pitch of your voice changes from syllable to syllable. Since this is a question, the last couple of words were probably in the upper range of pitch.

Ask this question out loud ten times in a row, saying it exactly the same way each time. What do you notice about the sound? After the third or fourth time, it sounds like something more sung than spoken. This is because the various pitches have become familiar—you begin to anticipate how they will sound. Try it again, slowing down the rhythm, and listen to how musical this spoken question becomes after only a few repetitions.

In everyday speaking, we use a variety of pitch levels, from low to high. Think about how you would say to someone, "Stop!" if he or she were about to step out in front of a moving car. Now compare that to how you would ask someone to join you for dinner. "Stop!" would probably be in the upper part of your declamatory voice and higher in pitch than "Would you like to have dinner?," which is likely to be relaxed, conversational, and lower. Pitch fluctuates within every sentence we speak, sometimes within every word.

Pitch and intensity do not always go hand in hand, however: Each is produced in a different way. If the vocal folds transfer all of the passing breath into actual sound, a moderately loud tone, typical of normal speaking or singing, is produced. However, if too much breath is allowed to escape unused, the voice will release a breathy, quiet tone. If the vocal folds are too tightly positioned, the result is a forced, constricted sound.

While intensity is dependent upon proximity of the vocal folds, actual pitch is determined by coordinating tiny muscles within the larynx. The more frequent the vibrations per second, the higher the tone; the less frequent, the lower the tone. Therefore, higher doesn't necessarily mean louder, nor does lower always mean softer, in spite of what the natural tendency may be.

Following is an exercise that will enable you to explore the way in which your breath and vocal folds work together dynamically. It is best performed with a group of four or more people. Be sure to follow the directions carefully.

Full Circle Sing: A Group Exercise

Stand in a large circle, two to three feet apart, with everyone facing inward. Close your eyes and completely relax your body, balancing your weight on the balls of your feet. The exercise begins spontaneously with an undesignated member of the circle—whoever has the impulse to start.

The beginner chooses a pitch and vowel sound (*oh, ah, ee,* etc.) in the middle part of her voice. As soon as the first sound is established, all other members of the circle join in and match the pitch and vowel sound as closely as possible. Each person in the circle sustains this sound for one full breath, whether or not it coincides with other members of the group. At the end of a breath, each member begins a new vowel on a different pitch in a different part of her register.

With each new sound, participants should explore both low and high registers of the voice. Since everyone's breath capacity is different, the original sound will gradually fade away as new sounds are introduced. The exercise may last several minutes and will likely stop itself.

This exercise is useful in that it enables you to explore your voice in a setting of complete freedom. Once everyone has established individual sounds, a wonderful conglomeration of harmonics is created. I find that beginning singers are prone to make sounds in a circle like this that they would never consider making with a voice instructor or in front of a group of people. It is extremely liberating and informative.

While each member of the circle should be aware of the overall sound in this exercise, close attention should be paid to the way individual sounds feel. Where do they vibrate in the body? In what way do lower sounds feel different than higher sounds? A discussion should follow the exercise with each person describing his or her personal experience.

The next exercise can be done in a group or alone in a quiet room.

The Sustained Word

Lie comfortably on the floor and relax your body completely. Close your eyes and think of a one-syllable word. Choose one that is friendly and pleasant-sounding to you, creating a calming image in your mind. Speak the word out loud, over and over, saying it exactly the same way each time.

Take a breath between each repetition. Make sure you say the word in a comfortable, middle part of your range, careful not to speak too low in pitch.

After three or four times, begin to speak the word more slowly. Gradually slow the rhythm of your speaking until it takes one entire breath to say the word. Be sure and speak it with the same inflection each time.

Once you use the entire breath to speak the word, gradually increase your speed until you're back to normal.

This exercise illustrates how singing really is a sustained form of speech. You cannot help but sing as you decrease the speed with which you speak the word.

Singing differs from speaking in that it requires you to be specific about pitch and to sustain your action over a longer period of time. Everyday speaking is spontaneous, produced naturally with an impulse that occurs only millimoments before sound is produced, but in acting and singing, the text is prescribed, and impulse is easily lost. This prompts us to keenly observe our everyday impulses so that we may re-create them on stage. Once this happens, in either speech or song, we live truthfully.

Exercises in this chapter have been designed to help you discover and explore some of the basic elements of your singing voice. I encourage you to go back and do them again. Wait at least a day before reading on and allow yourself to ponder what you've discovered. Moving too quickly through the process can lead to unnecessary frustration. Once you've settled into your voice through these exercises, you can learn more about what you've just discovered—that you are indeed a singer!

The chapters that follow will offer some insight into the specifics of what you've just experienced. Understand that discussions of vocal technique range from highly technical to oversimplified. In an effort to avoid confusion, I will simplify the process as much as possible without misleading the reader. Hence, some of the descriptions that follow may not be one

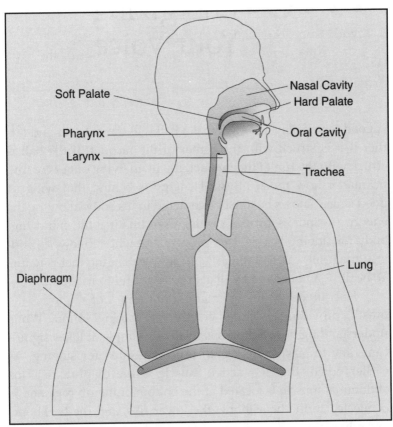

Figure 5–1. Front view of the major structures of the singing voice.

hundred percent accurate in the strictest physiological sense. Too much information too soon, especially from a book, often creates diminishing returns.

Remember to focus not only on the physiology of technique, but on the experiences that are created by it. Avoid precisionistic manipulation of muscles and focus on the attending sensations of what is described. Singing is a deceptively simple act.

...6 ∎Energizing Your Voice

A good tennis player knows that a ball will travel faster and farther if it is struck with the center of the racquet. If the ball is struck with the rim of the racquet, it will go flying out of control, no matter how much physical energy is behind the swing. A good singer knows he must be centered in his body, allowing the energy to find its proper origin. Coordinating the mind and body for singing is a delicate process, but when followed properly, the result can feel remarkably simple. Singing that is natural, healthy, and centered will also be beautiful to listen to.

Unequivocally, the most important aspect of singing is the breath, providing essential energy for making sound. While understanding how it works is relatively simple, it takes significant time to master the breath process needed for singing. As earlier noted, the first active muscle is the diaphragm. This abdominal muscle is located at the bottom of the rib cage and is connected to the breastbone, the lower ribs, and the backbone, extending upward in a dome shape where it connects to the lower portion of the lungs. The diaphragm is lower in the back than in the front, matching the shape of the rib cage.

Upon impulse, the diaphragm moves downward, forcing muscles and organs in the abdominal area (the stomach) to protrude. Many singers assume it is the diaphragm that protrudes, but it doesn't descend that low, nor can it be seen or felt. When the abdominal muscles are held and unable to protrude naturally, they prevent the diaphragm from lowering completely and limit the amount of air taken into the lungs. Holding the abdominal muscles in during inspiration also forces the motion of the breath up into the chest cavity. This is commonly called "chest breathing" and is the most common form of inefficient breath management.

Even if the abdominal muscles are relaxed, poor body alignment can still cause chest breathing to happen. If the chest cavity is not in an upright position, or slumped over even slightly, the abdominal muscles must compensate by forcing the rib cage upward. Substantial movement in the chest cavity during the inhalation process is a sign of resistance to the breath.

The importance of relaxing the abdominal muscles when breath drops into the body cannot be overstated. Many singers are taught to flex or extend these muscles. This approach not only wastes energy, it severely limits a singer's breath capacity. Some teachers suggest that students try to feel the breath entering the body from the pelvic area in order to relax these muscles completely. The lower the singer can feel movement during inspiration, the more efficiently the breath is managed.

As infants, most of us naturally breathed in this manner, though we were never instructed so. Unfortunately, our infant bodies grow quickly and ideas of posture and breathing become greatly influenced by outside forces. As children, many of us learn poor breathing habits during elementary school, where we spend most of the hours of the day leaning over a desk or table. In this position, the body cannot maximize its use of breath because it is not properly aligned. When we mature into adults and begin to study voice, we have to modify aspects of our alignment and breathing that may be counterproductive.

Proper *breath management* is dependent on physical alignment and is the foundation of healthy singing. For decades, teachers of singing have used the term *breath support* to describe what is needed to fuel a sound. But this is a misnomer—the singing voice is actually supported by the physical body, not the breath. Once the body is properly aligned, the breath enables the body to produce a fully supported sound. If the body is not properly aligned, certain muscles are forced to compensate for each other, causing tension and strain.

Relaxation and Alignment

The following exercises will help you properly align the body and breathe in the manner needed for healthy singing. Performing on stage will not always lend itself to this posture.

However, like any element of technique, practicing it religiously will condition the muscles to respond efficiently on their own. If we go to the gym in the morning, we don't spend the rest of the day trying to actively benefit from our workout. We go, we exercise, and we forget about it. The same must happen with vocal technique: do the exercises and *forget about them on stage*. The most common downfall of the singer in performance is his own awareness of technique.

These exercises should be done with a teacher or friend who can read the instructions and monitor your response. If you are alone, you may want to tape-record them so you can follow directions freely (lengthy pauses should come between each sentence of the exercise, allowing you ample time to respond). Many relaxation exercises done on the floor tend to put the mind and body to sleep. While doing them, it's important to remember that as relaxation increases, so should awareness.

Exercise in Relaxation and Awareness

1. Lie on the floor with a medium-size book (300–400 pages) behind your head. Be sure that your feet are shoulder-width apart and that your arms lie fully extended at your sides.
2. Close your eyes. Allow the breath to enter and leave your body quietly through the nose and mouth.
3. Allow your mind to travel down to the area of your toes. Wiggle and flex them vigorously as your breath drops in; relax them completely as breath is released. Imagine your toes floating away from your body.
4. Move your feet in a circular motion at the ankles as your breath drops in, and relax them as breath is released. Imagine they, too, have left your body.
5. Flex the calf muscles of the lower legs as your breath drops in, relax them as breath is released.
6. Flex the buttocks as breath drops in; relax them as breath is released.

7. Notice the natural curve of your spine, allow it to rest comfortably in this position. Imagine a warm, powerful energy traveling from the tailbone to the neck, massaging and relaxing every vertebra of the spine as you allow the breath in.

8. Flex the muscles in the shoulder area a few times as your breath enters your body, and imagine the muscles floating away as breath is released.

9. Notice how heavy your arms seem to be on the floor against the pull of gravity. Flex the muscles in your arms a few times as you allow the breath to drop in; release them with the breath.

10. Wiggle your fingers as the breath drops in; imagine them floating away as breath is released.

11. Imagine your arms and hands are completely disconnected from the rest of the body, floating away.

12. Stretch and scrunch the muscles in your face and jaw a few times as the breath drops in, releasing them completely with the breath.

13. Now imagine that you're floating above your physical body, which you've left behind on the floor, completely disconnected from your mind.

14. In this state, observe your natural breathing: its rhythm, its depth, and its natural speed. Don't rush the time you take between breaths. Focus on the breath completely.

15. Relax the abdominal muscles. As breath drops into the body, they move outward. As breath is released, so are the muscles.

16. Allow the muscles in your lower back to expand as well, bringing that area of your body closer to the floor as breath drops in.

17. Remain in this state for five minutes, observing the natural breath of your body. Where is there movement? Where is there no movement? Remember, as your relaxation increases, so should your awareness.

Nearly everyone will breathe deeply while doing the above exercise the first time. Note that when you're on your back, the abdominal muscles move outward each time the breath drops in, and relax as the breath is released. Once the entire body is relaxed, this is the only movement that takes place.

The next exercise demonstrates how this posture can be found on your feet. Take a five-minute break before moving on.

Abdominal Breathing Exercise

1. Stand in the middle of the room with your feet shoulder-width apart.
2. As your breath naturally enters your body, slowly raise extended arms up over your head in "snow-angel" or "airplane" fashion. If the abdominal muscles are completely relaxed, you may feel that your breath is not as deep as before. This is normal.
3. As breath is released from your body, slowly lower your arms back to your sides while keeping your chest cavity comfortably high.
4. Roll your shoulders forward and backward, feeling that they are simply hanging from your body.
5. Allow breath to enter and leave your body through your nose and mouth.
6. Allow the breath to expand your abdominal area in the front and lower back.
7. Find a focal point across the room that is eye level, being careful not to allow your head to drop too far forward or backward. Gently place your hands on your navel as before.
8. Notice how your hands move outward as breath drops in and how they relax inward as breath is released.
9. Don't press on your stomach with your hands; just let them rest there. Observe your breathing in this position for several minutes.

While it may feel like the breath is filling up your belly, it can only go in and out of the lungs. Remember that the diaphragm is causing the stomach to move outward.

Proper alignment of the neck and head is essential to allowing breath to enter and leave the body freely. A common alignment error is to have the head tilted too far back. Tilting back can constrict the flow of breath through the trachea and put a strain on the larynx. Spotting a point on the wall across the room that is eye level is always a good idea.

If you observe your chest moving significantly upward as your breath drops in, your body may not be properly aligned or relaxed. There are usually two reasons for this: (1) the chest area is not comfortably high before the breath is allowed to drop into the body, and (2) the abdominal muscles are not relaxed, creating pressure against the diaphragm as it tries to move downward. If the chest area is already in a heightened position, then it does not need to move upward when the breath drops in. If you discover movement in the chest, check your alignment by raising your arms over your head, then lowering them while keeping the chest comfortably high.

Finding the relaxation needed in the abdominal area may not come easily at first. Repeat the above exercises until free abdominal breathing is in place. It may help to allow the breath to pass through the nose initially, opening the mouth after the breath begins to drop in. It is also useful to think of the breath as entering the body through the pelvic region. The lower the movement, the better. Take a break before moving on.

Expanding Your Breath

The breath process described in the previous section is normal, everyday breathing for life. In order to establish good habits for singing, we must build on this process and cultivate a greater awareness of the muscles being used, especially during the release.

Previously, the breath left the body very quickly. A more conscious control over the release, however, enables the breath to leave the body more slowly and economically. The way in which the muscles are used during the release determines how long a sound can be sustained.

Many beginning students of singing find that they are not able to sustain the breath on a sung or spoken sound for very long. This leads to an oversimplified solution: that the lungs can be trained to take in more air and therefore have more air to release. This is only half true. While some expansion of the lungs will be experienced over time and prove to be helpful, it is not the only key to sustaining long sounds.[1]

There are essentially two factors that govern the duration of released breath: (1) how the muscles in the abdominal region are activated, and (2) how the release is measured by the vocal folds.

If the rib cage and lungs are allowed to collapse quickly during the release, the resultant sound is anemic and short. If the rib cage is held comfortably high and expanded during the release, however, the breath is economized. At the same time, the vocal folds and artic-ulators—lips, teeth, and tongue—provide resistance to the breath. A breath that is released too quickly will create a shorter sound, but a breath that is paced properly can create a much longer one.

The exercises that follow are designed to expand the amount of breath that enters and leaves the body and to help you begin managing it more efficiently. It is essential that all pre-vious exercises be mastered first.

Suspending the Breath

1. With proper physical alignment, allow the breath to drop into the body, relaxing the abdominal area.
2. Once the lungs have reached a comfortably full capacity, "suspend" the breath by simply stopping the impulse to inhale any further. Don't redirect the breath and "hold" it with a closed larynx, as you would under water; just stop the motion of the breath and remain still for a few seconds.
3. Release the breath slowly.

---

1. It should be pointed out that the extent of expansion in the lungs and abdominal area is influenced by the singer's cardiovascular condition. A performer who partic-ipates in some sort of aerobic exercise on a daily basis is naturally going to find a greater capacity for breath than one who is more sedentary in nature.

The purpose of suspending the breath is to find greater expansion in the abdominal region, not to literally prepare for the sound. For the purposes of increasing expansion, we'll elongate it. The exercise below follows the suspension with an audible sound.

Suspension and Natural Release

1. Stand comfortably in the middle of the room, properly aligned. Allow the breath to drop in comfortably as in the previous exercises.
2. Suspend the breath for five counts.
3. Slowly release the breath on a quiet, sustained hissing sound. Allow your abdominal area to feel like a balloon with a small leak, releasing the air very slowly. Be sure that you're not "holding back" your breath in order to achieve a longer release—allow resistance to happen naturally in the mouth.

You may notice that the release of your breath is longer now because it met with resistance from the teeth and tongue. Practice this exercise several times before continuing. After a few repetitions, you may feel slightly dizzy. Don't panic; this is normal. If this happens, relax your entire body by sitting or squatting for a few minutes before going on.

Suspension and Active Release

1. Stand comfortably in the middle of the room, properly aligned. Allow the breath to drop in all around as before.
2. Suspend the breath for five counts.
3. Release the breath on a hiss. Allow it to be consistent, smooth, and slow.
4. Allow the abdominal area to flex more and more as the breath is released. Remain active until the lungs are emptied.

Note that while the abdominal muscles are completely relaxed during inspiration, they are now more active (slightly flexed, not protruded) during the release of the breath. Take a pause between breaths to ensure that these muscles have the opportunity to relax each time. Remember that chest breathing can happen if these muscles are not relaxed when the breath drops in.

The more you do these exercises in one sitting, the more tired your body will become. If you reach a point of diminishing returns at any point, stop and take a lengthy break or come back to the exercises later.

The following exercise will help keep the rib cage expanded while activating the abdominal muscles.

Belt Exercise

1. Take a belt or a piece of elastic and place it around the rib cage just below the breasts. Make sure it is snug and doesn't slip down the abdomen.

2. Raise your arms out to your side and over your head so that the chest becomes comfortably high. Notice the sense of fullness in the chest as it pushes against the belt. Try to maintain this fullness as the arms are slowly lowered. Relax the shoulders.

3. You may notice that the abdominal muscles are flexed now, particularly if you are trying to fill out the chest area behind the belt. Relax these muscles completely while keeping the chest comfortably high. You may notice the tightness in the belt decrease a little.

4. Now release the breath on a quiet, sustained hiss as before. Try to maintain the fullness in the rib cage behind the belt as long as possible by flexing the abdominal muscles. Note that the fullness can also be felt in the lower back.

5. The abdominal muscles should gradually become more active as the breath is released.

6. Release the abdominal muscles and allow the breath to replenish naturally, being careful not to allow the chest area to collapse.

The feeling of expansion in the rib cage cannot be sustained throughout the release; the rib cage will naturally collapse as abdominal muscles tire. The longer this feeling is maintained, however, the more freedom the lungs have to release the breath freely.

It's important to realize that the end of one breath is the beginning of the next. All the active muscles used in the release of the breath must immediately relax in order for the breath to drop back in. Now you're ready to make a vocalized sound.

Buzzing Release
1. Repeat the previous exercise, releasing the sound on a sustained z in the middle part of your voice.
2. Make sure the rib cage remains expanded for as long as possible.
3. When the breath is spent, relax the abdominal muscles and allow the lungs to be replenished.
4. Repeat.

By using a z sound, we engage the vocal folds, thereby increasing resistance of the breath. When the breath meets with greater resistance from the vocal cords, it is measured more efficiently.

It's crucial that the abdominal muscles remain relaxed during inhalation in any of the above exercises. Simply relaxing these muscles will cause the breath to drop in automatically. Remember that proper inhalation happens naturally, it is not manipulated in any way. Breathing also requires a recovery period at the end of each release. If you have a tendency to rush into the next breath, remember that the body must completely relax first.

It's also important that the shoulders not be pulled back. This usually happens when you try to keep the ribs expanded. Guard against this tendency by always keeping the shoulders relaxed. You can monitor them by rolling them forward or backward slightly at any time.

For maximum results, you should do the exercises in this chapter daily so that your muscles are trained to respond in the most efficient manner possible. Spend no more than ten minutes a day with breathing exercises, however. If you feel tired and are no longer making progress, simply quit.

Summary of Breath Management

- Proper physical alignment is essential to efficient breath management.
- The chest area must be comfortably high before, during, and after the release of the breath.
- The abdominal muscles are completely relaxed when the breath drops in and become active when sound is produced.
- The act of suspension enables you to find greater expansion in the abdominal region and to coordinate the muscles for singing before a sound is made. While suspending the breath should not be incorporated into a performance, it is a useful tool in the studio.
- The amount of breath available for release is not solely dependent on the apparent amount of breath taken in. Resistance from vocal folds and expansion of the rib cage economize the breath in the release.
- Less energy expended in the process of inhalation means more energy is available during the release.
- A brief moment of recovery is required before the next sound can be made.

■ ■ ■ 7 ■ Your Vocal Mechanism

The source of any sound, musical or otherwise, is vibration: guitar strings vibrate when plucked, cymbals vibrate when struck with a mallet—even the sound of a heavy book being dropped on a hard surface is created by vibration. Sounds made by the human voice are generated by vibrations in the vocal folds. The vocal folds are located in the larynx (pronounced *LAIR-inks*) at the top of the trachea (see Figure 5–1 on page 35). While the larynx initiates spoken or sung sounds, its primary purpose is to keep food, drink, and other extraneous matter from entering the lungs. This is why speaking and swallowing must remain mutually exclusive events!

The vocal folds have strong muscles that control the flow of breath, allowing it either to pass freely or to become partially or completely stopped. When the vocal folds are positioned close enough together, passing breath causes them to vibrate, creating sound. This is much like the effect achieved when a balloon full of air is released, causing the mouth to vibrate and make a funny sound. If we hold the mouth of a balloon full of air in a taut position, we can regulate the sound it makes by stretching it out (making the pitch higher) or relaxing it (making it lower). It's the vibration in the mouth of the balloon that creates the sound. Although the vocal mechanism is made up of much more complex muscles than a balloon might suggest, the process is very similar.

In general, the number of muscles used to activate the vocal mechanism far outweigh the number used in the breathing process. In fact, the act of speaking or singing requires more muscles than most any other human activity. Just like the lungs, diaphragm, and ribs, we can train these muscles to respond in ways that are more productive for speaking or singing.

Approaching a Sound

There are essentially three stages of any vocal sound: *onset, sustain,* and *release.* The onset (also called *phonation*) is the point at which breath and the vocal folds are met to produce a sound. This is the most important phase of a sound because it establishes conditions for what will follow.

Take a moment to make a few recurring *hh* sounds with your voice.[1] Don't form any particular vowel sound, just allow aspirated breath to be released. Do it again, varying the intensity of the sound from loud to soft. Notice the sensation created when you attempt to make the sound quietly; compare that to what it takes to make the louder one. For the louder sound, the vocal folds are closer together, and more breath passes through them. The breath and vocal folds work dynamically with the muscles in the larynx to create the intensity of the sound and the exact pitch.

Now make a few *ha* sounds in a row. How do these sounds compare with the loudest *hh* sound you made earlier? You will notice that even more energy is required for a vocalized *ha.* This energy is a combination of increased breath and additional muscles of the vocal mechanism being engaged.

Now make the *ha* sound in slow motion. Move from the quiet *hh* sound as gradually as possible into the actual *ah* part of the sound. Notice the gradual increase from a breathy sound to one that is fully engaged with a sense of pitch. Sounds that do not produce pitch, like the aspirant *h*, are referred to as *unvoiced* or *voiceless*, while sounds that produce pitch, like the *ah*, are *voiced*.

There is a variety of ways in which the vocal folds and the breath can be coordinated. In the above example, you've already demonstrated one: the *soft onset.* The soft onset occurs when the breath arrives in the larynx *before* the vocal folds come close enough together to make a pitched sound. The breath passes

1. Since not all readers will be familiar with the International Phonetic Alphabet, I have made a conscious choice not to use it. As a result, certain sounds will not be in their purest form. All actors and singers are advised to become familiar with IPA, as it is invaluable to the process of understanding and replicating particular sounds in spoken dialects and singing.

through the vocal folds, creating the *h* part of the sound first. As the vocal folds come closer together, they gradually begin to vibrate, creating the *ah* part of the sound you just demonstrated. This closure of the vocal folds is often referred to as *approximation*.

The soft onset is useful primarily in singing words that begin with an *h* sound, like *have, how,* and *heaven*. Even when these words occur in the middle of a sung phrase, the vocal folds have to be in a position that is slightly apart for the first portion of the sound, moving closer together to create the rest of the syllable or word. This sound is generally not desirable in singing because it allows too much breath to pass through the vocal folds, creating a breathy, anemic tone that seems shallow and unsupported. While it is necessary at times, it is not the desired tone in general.

At the other end of the continuum lies the *plosive onset*. This sound, sometimes called a *glottal stop* or *hard attack*, is created when the vocal folds are approximated *before* the breath arrives. In this case, the breath is barricaded by the vocal folds and then suddenly released in an "explosive" manner.

Experiment with a plosive onset by grunting an *uh* sound several times in a row. This is the same sound produced when you lift something heavy. Notice the absence of breathiness in the onset of this sound. If any breath is heard at all, it's at the *end* of the sound. Make this sound a few times in slow motion. Notice how the vocal folds seem to grind the sound out as they are forced apart by the breath. This sound is useful only to a point in singing, usually to separate or articulate vowel sounds and only in certain circumstances.

The type of onset used affects the quality of the sound that follows it, thereby setting the tone (pun intended) for an entire word or phrase. Extremities like the soft onset or hard attack can be detrimental to the resultant tone, especially in singing, and can lead to vocal tension and fatigue.

A good singer strives for a sound that lies more toward the middle of the continuum: the *balanced onset*. This balance occurs when the breath arrives in the larynx *at the same time* as the vocal folds are approximated. This requires coordinating the breath with the positioning of the vocal folds simultaneously. Practicing a balanced onset will ensure that you don't under- or overenergize your breath, thereby preserving the health of your voice.

Begin to create a balanced onset by saying the syllable *ah* a few times in a row. Think about the very first particle of sound as you produce it. It should be neither breathy nor plosive. Imagine a slight *h* before the vowel, but don't allow it to be audible. Notice how free and natural the onset is and how the quality of the *ah* is improved.

The exercises below are designed to cultivate a balanced onset. It should be pointed out that many people approach vocal production with a balanced onset naturally, so you may find this particular set of exercises a part of your normal production of sound. If so, guard against any tendencies to overcorrect. The various steps of each exercise in this chapter are designed to happen quickly, moving from one step to the next without interruption. It will be helpful to study an exercise from beginning to end and memorize it before attempting it.

Soft to Plosive Onset

1. With proper physical alignment, allow the breath to drop in completely as in the previous chapter.
2. Suspend the breath for two counts.
3. In the middle part of your range, say the ah vowel ten times in a steady rhythm (not too fast). Begin with a soft onset and, with each repetition, gradually increase the approximation of your vocal folds until you've reached the plosive on the tenth onset.
4. Between each onset, allow the breath to be replenished by simply relaxing the abdominal muscles.
5. You should reach a perfectly balanced onset on or around the fifth release.
6. Maintain the expansion of the rib cage as much as possible throughout.

Notice the infinite range of onsets that can be created depending on how closely approximated the vocal folds are. Given this fact, the balanced onset is not just one point but a range of acceptable ones.

The Balanced Onset

1. With proper physical alignment, allow the breath to drop in completely, releasing the muscles in the abdominal area.
2. Suspend the breath for two counts.
3. In the middle part of your range, say the *ah* vowel ten times, striving for a balanced onset each time.
4. Maintain the expansion of the rib cage as much as possible throughout.

You may find yourself veering toward the soft or plosive onset from time to time. If so, adjust the sound on the next release. The rib cage and lower abdominal muscles will seem to pulse slightly on each sound if the body is properly aligned.

In actual performance, your thoughts cannot actively be directed toward the type of onset you're using. As with breath management, practicing the balanced onset in the studio religiously will train the vocal mechanism to respond in the most efficient manner possible in performance.

The exercise below demonstrates how a balanced onset can improve the quality of sound that follows it. You'll be using the first phrase of the children's song "Are You Sleeping, Brother John?" ("Frère Jacques"). You can use any simple song that begins with a vowel sound, however.

Balanced Onset in a Musical Phrase

1. With proper physical alignment, allow the breath to drop in completely, releasing the muscles in the abdominal area.
2. Suspend the breath for two counts.

3. In a comfortable part of your range, sing the first phrase, "Are you sleeping, are you sleeping," in one breath. Begin with a soft onset, using lots of *h* at the beginning of the first word. Notice how the entire phrase seems breathy and unsupported.

4. Next, sing the phrase beginning with a plosive onset, allowing the air to "explode" on the first sound. Notice the harsh quality of the entire phrase based on the type of onset used.

5. Sing the phrase again, in one breath, beginning with a balanced onset. Imagine a slight *h* before the first sound, but don't allow it to become audible. Notice how full and supported the entire phrase seems to be, all based on the onset of the first sound.

Remember that while there are times when a soft or plosive onset is required, neither should become the norm. Striving for the balanced onset while building technique will allow soft and plosive approaches to occur naturally when needed.

Many beginning singers will produce a balanced onset naturally. If you feel for some reason that you lean toward a soft or hard onset, go back and repeat the exercises a few times until you begin to find a balance between breath and your vocal mechanism. Once you've mastered the balanced onset, continue.

Sustaining a Sound

The second phase of a sound is the sustained portion itself. The *sustain* begins immediately after the onset and is present until the sound is released. How long this portion lasts depends on the music you're singing. The sustain phase should be steady and consistent. Aside from seeming to move forward with energy and vitality, it does not change once it is established. The lips, teeth, and tongue are active in shaping or releasing the sound, but they do not alter it. The breath is what keeps the sound consistent, and if it wavers or comes in surges, the sound will be altered and uneven. In order to ensure an evenness of breath, the body must be properly aligned and a feeling of expanding the rib cage maintained.

There exist many concepts and ideas on how to sustain a sound successfully. When asked how she sustains such long notes in her recordings, Barbra Streisand once commented that she "wills" herself to hold them out. While this may seem to oversimplify the process, there is some truth here. Like the act of singing itself, a singer who doesn't believe he can sustain a note for very long will seldom do so. A simple determination to measure the breath can produce wonderful results.

Sustaining a long tone, as mentioned earlier, is not the result of using less breath: holding back breath means wasting it. If this were not the case, we could hold our breath for as long as we wanted. In fact, using more breath enables you to sustain notes longer. Here's why: Remember that breath and vocal folds work dynamically together to create a sound, both in terms of intensity and pitch. The same is true for measuring the breath: the more breath that passes through approximated vocal folds, the more fuel they have to work with. In simplest of terms, you must first generate breath in order to manage it efficiently. (It's like spending money in order to make it or like being in an Equity show before getting your card, only much less frustrating than either of these.)

The expanded rib cage is a valuable tool for sustaining a sound. When the rib cage is expanded all around, you experience a feeling of buoyancy and size, very similar to that of the breathing-in process. Since this expansion is necessary for sustaining sounds, it can be helpful to think of yourself as breathing in, while sustaining a tone, or that breath somehow remains inside your body, even though it is leaving it. In other words, use more breath, but think less breath.

The amount of usable breath available to us at any given point is also dynamically connected to how much physical exertion is going on. If we're exercising or dancing in a number on stage, for example, we have less breath available for speaking or singing. Overextending ourselves physically while sustaining a sound will reduce the available amount of breath. This is why you should feel complete and total relaxation in the vocal mechanism, the shoulders, and any other part of the body that is prone to become active in sustaining a sound. If any feeling of "work" is experienced, it should be felt in the abdominal region.

The exercise below is designed to increase your ability to sustain a sung sound.

The Sustained Word II

1. Choose a single-syllable word that creates a calming image in your mind; you may even use the same one used in the exercise in Chapter 5.
2. With proper physical alignment, allow the breath to drop in and the abdominal region to naturally expand.
3. Using a balanced onset, speak the word slowly and release any unused breath gently.
4. On a new breath, repeat the word, speaking it much more slowly. Linger on the vowel sound in the middle of the word. Release the remainder of the breath.
5. Now use an entire breath to speak the word, sustaining the vowel sound for as long as possible. Remember to start with a balanced onset.
6. As you sustain the sound, keep the rib cage expanded as long as possible. Remember that it will naturally begin to collapse about halfway through the sustain.
7. Rest before repeating.

Since you were speaking this word and not singing it, you may have fluctuated somewhat in terms of pitch. Go back and do the exercise again, but allow the vowel sound of the word to remain constant in terms of both quality and pitch. Strive to keep the sound vital and full of life, always moving it forward.

Explore different areas of your voice in doing this exercise, singing in the upper, middle, and lower registers. This exercise will tire the body if repeated more than three or four times at once, creating the feeling that no progress is being made. Be sure to give yourself ample resting time between repetitions. Mastering this simple aspect of sustaining a sound will be a fundamental building block for the future development of your voice. There are many other exercises in sustaining a sound that involve specific musical patterns and are best done with a teacher at the piano. As with any aspect of vocal technique, qualified mentoring is essential.

Releasing a Sound

The final stage of a sound is the *release*. This moment is as instantaneous as the onset and contributes to the response your voice will have when making the next sound. While continuity between the onset and release of a sound is often easily maintained, it is possible to begin a sound properly, yet release it poorly.

If the vocal folds separate before the breath is stopped, a *soft release* occurs. Similar to the soft onset, the soft release is breathy and unsupported. Frequently, untrained singers have a habit of realeasing a sound gradually, allowing the breath to fade away. Some will think this release is more expressive or more pleasant to listen to, but in reality it creates an anemic sound that is unsupported and often below the pitch. To prevent this from happening, the sustained portion of a sound should continue with full energy until the point of the release; there should be no doubt as to the exact point at which the sound stops.

Similarly, if the breath is stopped before the vocal folds separate (causing them to close completely), a *hard release* occurs. This sound will have the tendency to be cut off or choked and can cause unnecessary strain on the vocal mechanism. Singers who are prone to sing too loudly are often disposed to a hard release—grunting out the final moment. This is further evidence that onset, sustain, and release are dynamically connected.

One obstacle that frequently occurs at the point of a release is the final consonant. Because many consonants cannot be sustained and because all are produced with less space in the mouth than vowels, the tendency is to create a hard release in an effort to "sing" the final consonant. While the final consonant is important and should be clearly present, it will often cause the singer to anticipate the release of a word and to close the preceding vowel prematurely. The same can be true for diphthongs—two consecutive vowel sounds in the same syllable—where singers tend to close the second vowel too quickly.

Diphthongs and final consonants should be placed exactly at the point of release without regard to what has been happening previously. The final sound of a phrase should be thought of as the release itself. If a word ends in a vowel, it should be released as though a consonant were present and not by fading away the breath, although in certain dramatic situations, "rules" like this can be broken but only because the actor chooses. It is best for a singer to think of the entire vocal instrument—vocal folds, breath, teeth, lips, and tongue—as relaxing simultaneously, creating a *balanced release*. The mouth should remain open after the release occurs, even if the final consonant requires a closed mouth. Opening the mouth at the end of a sound will help prepare you for the next impulse of breath. The following exercise will help establish a balanced release:

Laughing Release

1. With proper alignment, allow the breath to drop in while relaxing the abdominal muscles.
2. Suspend the breath for two counts.
3. Deliver a genuine laugh: *ha ha ha ha ha*. Do this several times and observe the release of each vowel.
4. Repeat the laugh slower and slower each time, allowing small breaths to drop in between each *ha*.
5. If the release of one *ha* is the breath for the next, then the release is balanced.
6. Sustain the final *ha* for a few seconds and simply stop the breath to release it.

In this simple exercise are all the components needed for healthy production of sound: proper alignment and breath management, a balanced onset, consistency in sustaining the vowel (however short), and a balanced release. Further exercises can be explored in releasing a tone as well, all with a qualified teacher and the aid of a piano.

Summary of the Vocal Mechanism

- The vocal folds and muscles in the larynx work dynamically with the breath to control the volume and pitch of a sound.
- There are three stages to a vocal sound: onset, sustain, and release.
- While soft and plosive onsets are useful, singers should strive for a balanced onset as the normal production of sound. When either the soft or plosive approach becomes the standard, the vocal mechanism is strained.
- The sustained portion of a sound should be consistent in quality and is dependent on both a balanced onset and the expansion of abdominal muscles.
- Sustaining a long note is not the result of using less breath. Breath that is held back is wasted. Using more breath enables you to sustain notes longer because the vocal folds have more fuel to measure and sustain.
- The release of a sound is as instantaneous as the onset and establishes conditions for the next approach.
- A singer should strive for a balanced release, not one that is choked or faded away by breath.
- Words or phrases that end in a vowel sound should be released as though a consonant were present.
- The mouth should always remain open after the release of a sound.

▪ ▪ ▪ 8 ▪ Resonance: Your Acoustics

As outlined in the previous chapter, the vocal mechanism is the source of any spoken or sung sound; however, the sound produced here is basically neutral, nonspecific. Once the sound leaves the mechanism, it is modified to form a syllable or word. The first stage of this process is called *resonance*.

The term *resonate* is derived from the word *resound*, meaning to ring or echo. Sound waves resound or "bounce around" in the environment in which they are produced. Much like a basketball on a gym floor, each bounce will prompt another until the energy is eventually spent. A large room with hard surfaces serves as a resonator for sounds by enabling vibrations to bounce back and forth from many different points. This unique effect is called *acoustics*. When the human voice is activated, sound waves bounce around acoustic chambers within the body, creating resonance.

In addition to shaping distinguishable sound, resonators expand the size and quality of the sound into something more pleasant to listen to. They also act as monitors for vocal technique, enabling us to re-create certain desirable sensations. Without some sort of vibration in the resonating chambers, we would know very little about how we sound to others.

The size, shape, and surface of a resonating chamber are all major factors in determining how vibrations behave within it. In general, larger resonators reflect and amplify lower pitches while smaller ones respond to higher tones. A soft, spongy surface such as carpet in a room tends to absorb a sound, while a harder surface such as a wooden floor tends to reflect a sound. There are a variety of shapes and surfaces to the resonators within your body, each working together to create your unique vocal quality.

Resonance in the Chest

The chest is the lowest and largest resonator. It tends to reflect lower tones more than higher ones, which explains why everyday speech tends to resonate there. In spite of these strong vibrations, chest resonance has little to do with the external quality of sound. While it's a strong indicator of full vocal function, it is not that useful to the singer in terms of shaping a sound. This is because the chest cavity is below the vocal folds—remember that breath carries sound upward in the body.

Chest Resonance
1. Place your hand on your breastplate and make a few humming sounds at different pitch levels.
2. Speak the words *nine hundred ninety-nine* in a relatively high part of your voice.
3. Now speak the same words in a low, comfortable register and notice how the vibration in the chest increases.

Chest resonance is virtually imperceptible to the listener, but it provides valuable feedback for the singer in the process of developing technique.

Resonance in the Throat

The throat or pharynx (pronounced *FAIR-inks*) is perhaps the most important resonator, simply because of its position, size, and flexibility (see Figure 5–1 on page 35). It is adjustable in size and shape, making it useful for amplifying both upper and lower tones. It is also the first chamber to receive sound vibrations after they leave the larynx. Unlike the chest, the pharynx is not directly connected to the larynx by cartilage or bone, so the vibrations it receives—carried freely on the breath—can be modified in many useful ways.

The pharynx has two major sections: oral and nasal. The

nasal portion begins in the nasal cavity and extends backward in the head, then downward to a point just above the tongue. Here, the soft palate (the soft part of the roof of the mouth near the back) is found. The oral portion of the pharynx begins just below the soft palate and extends down to a point just behind the larynx. Some sounds resonate in the nasal pharynx, like *n*, *m*, and many French vowel sounds, but most sounds resonate in the oral pharynx. The nasal pharynx can be closed off as needed by raising the soft palate, which you do by expanding the space in the throat.

In singing, the pharynx must be as open and relaxed as possible in order to achieve maximum resonance. An open throat enables the singer to tune and resonate a variety of pitches, high and low.

The Open Throat

1. Yawn a couple of times.
2. Notice what happens in the very first moments of a yawn: the throat opens completely and the soft palate is raised (judging by the cool spot you feel in the back of the mouth).
3. Move back and forth from normal throat posture to that created just prior to a yawn, but don't allow the yawn to happen.
4. With normal posture, say the word *hi* as you normally would to a friend.
5. With open posture—the very beginning of a yawn—say it again.
6. Switch back and forth several times and observe the difference in sound.
7. Now try saying *hi* with an open throat at various pitch levels in your voice. Notice how much more expansive a sound becomes when the throat is open.

Opening the throat in this way causes the larynx to be pulled downward. There is a tendency to confuse this process by activating the opposing set of muscles, which pull the larynx upward. These muscles are used in swallowing. Attempt to swallow and make a sound at the same time, and the conflict becomes obvious. Such a propensity is generally caused by tenseness or fear, creating a sound that is constricted or "held back."

It makes sense that a low-positioned larynx is ideal for singing, especially in the upper register, where the larynx tends to force itself upward. To compensate, the singer must maintain enough space in the throat, allowing the larynx to remain as low as possible. Remember that too much space, too much of a yawning feeling, will create unwanted tension.

The Oral Cavity

The oral cavity, or the mouth, is also a significant resonator because of its location, size and flexibility. In addition to providing resonance on sustained sounds, it is responsible for shaping sounds into words, using various articulators including the lips, teeth, and tongue.

Like the pharynx, the mouth must be kept relaxed and free of tension at all times to achieve optimum resonance. Given the fact that the articulators are constantly adjusting the sound for particular words, this can be difficult to maintain. The less effort exerted by the lips, teeth, and tongue, the more relaxed, open, and resonant the mouth will be. Maintaining an open throat will essentially free the muscles that control the articulators and create better resonance in the mouth.

The best way to maintain resonance in the mouth is to learn to produce vowel sounds correctly. Particular vowels will be discussed in the next chapter, but all are based on the simplest, most resonant sound, the neutral *uh*.

Neutral Vowel Posture
1. Observe the position of your mouth, teeth, lips, and tongue as they are right now.
2. You'll most likely find your tongue relatively flat and relaxed, with the tip resting behind the lower teeth.

3. Your lips are most likely closed. If this is the case, open the mouth slightly to a neutral position.
4. With this relaxed posture, simply activate the vocal folds with breath and sustain the sound that is naturally created.

The *uh* vowel is the most open and resonant of all, simply because it is the least manipulated. It is also the easiest to form because it is produced with the normal, at-rest posture described above.

The Nasal Cavity

The nasal cavity is important primarily in an articulatory sense: it enables us to sing *mm*, *nn*, and *ng* sounds as well as certain nasal sounds in foreign languages. The degree to which the nasal cavity is useful to the singer for other sounds is not universally agreed upon. Some theories tout its usefulness while others suggest it has no bearing on the tone whatsoever.

Some studies claim that singers who have colds do not produce a noticeably different quality than when they are well, providing the cold has not infected the vocal mechanism. They suggest that stuffed sinuses and nasal passages will create different sensations *inside* the body, causing the singer to feel that she does not sound her best, but to the outside listener the difference is imperceptible. While it's true that one can still produce a pleasant tone under these conditions, my experience shows that a difference in quality is detectable. While I may not notice a cold in the voice of someone I have never heard sing before, I am able to detect one in a student I hear sing on a regular basis. This suggests that a certain amount of nasal resonance is an essential part of a healthy tone.

There is also some question as to whether the nasal cavity actually resonates or simply receives sympathetic vibrations from the roof of the mouth (similar to the chest receiving vibrations from the larynx). For some sounds, the nasal cavity will vibrate even if the soft palate has closed it off.

Some performers have a propensity for a nasal sound, which means that the soft palate is allowing more vibrations to enter the nasal cavity than the oral cavity. While there may be disagreement as to how much nasality is required, one thing is clear: too much is too much.

Nasal Resonance

1. Say the syllable *mah* a couple of times. The posture of the vowel should feel much like the neutral *uh*.

2. Now elongate the syllable, lingering on the *mm* for a few moments before opening to the *ah*.

3. The *mm* clearly resonates in the nasal cavity—the mouth is closed, so it has no choice.

4. The placement of the *ah*, however, can vary. Speak *mah* again in slow motion and allow the *ah* to resonate in the same place as the *mm*. To do this, maintain the vibrations felt in the nose throughout the sound, allowing it to tickle. You'll notice an extremely nasal vowel sound.

5. Now speak/sing the syllable again in slow motion, but transfer the vibrations of the vowel sound to the roof of the mouth as the lips are parted. To do this, expand the throat in a pre-yawn position, raising the soft palate and closing off the nasal cavity.

You'll notice the amount of nasality in a sound can be controlled by transferring vibrations from the roof of the mouth to the nose. Though the transfer may seem to be a mental one, it is actually physically manipulated: the soft palate is raised and lowered by opening and relaxing the throat.

Terminology and Resonance

Because teachers of singing have varying opinions about the many aspects of resonance, terminology varies from one instructor to the next. Let's look at what some of the more common terms truly mean.

Based on the amount of vibration, a singer may feel that a sound is directed toward a particular area of the body. Many teachers, myself included, will ask students to "place" or "focus" a sound in a particular area in order to achieve the desired tone quality. The fact is that a sound cannot actually be placed anywhere in the body. Vibrations are the *result* of a sound being produced, not the source of it. Feeling that a sound is placed or focused in a particular region, however, may enable the singer to better adjust the muscles and resonators that effect that sound. Therefore, when a teacher and student discuss the *placement* of a particular sound, they must both understand how it relates to the sensations experienced by the student. Only after the student has first described the experience can a teacher communicate in terms that are understood.

Much of the external sound we hear from a singer is the result of all the resonating chambers combined, creating a unique tone quality. Sounds that teachers refer to as *dark* are generally produced by overexpanding the pharynx, preventing essential vibrations from entering the mouth. Similarly, sounds that are referred to as *bright* may indicate there is not enough expansion of the pharynx, thereby forcing vibrations to resonate outside the body rather than inside. This can be easily demonstrated on a stereo with treble and bass controls: the more bass added into the sound, the darker the quality; the more treble added, the brighter. Use of the terms *bright* and *dark* are helpful only when both student and teacher are aware of their true meanings.

An all-too-frequently used term for resonance is *projection*, one that should really be removed from our vocabularies. Contrary to popular belief, simply speaking or singing louder has little to do with being heard and understood. If a voice is not being allowed to resonate sufficiently in the body, no amount of volume is going to enable that sound to resonate in a large room—as with a stereo, increasing the volume does not improve the clarity of sound if treble and bass controls are mal-adjusted. Creating more vibrations *within* the body will lead to increased resonance *outside* the body. In many cases, an actor will simply try to sing or speak louder, especially when instructed to do so, and place undue strain on the voice. Not only does this fail to solve the problem, it leads to many a frustrated actor.

The tendency to use shortcut terminology like the ones mentioned here comes from the need to communicate quickly and efficiently. One of the marks of a good teacher (as outlined in Chapter 10) is the ability to develop a common language with a student. In this process, both the student and teacher are able to identify sensations or experiences with terms that are clearly understood by both. This is the foundation for successful mentoring.

Summary of the Resonance Process

- Resonating chambers within the body amplify and shape a sound.
- Primary resonators include the chest, pharynx (throat), oral cavity (mouth), and nasal cavity (nose).
- The chest cavity vibrates most in our everyday speaking. Lower tones tend to vibrate here, whereas higher tones tend to vibrate more in the head.
- Resonance in the pharynx has a significant bearing on the overall sound because of its position, size, and flexibility. Optimum resonance in the pharynx is similar to the first stages of a yawn.
- The oral cavity (mouth) is responsible for shaping sounds into syllables and words, particularly vowel sounds. The neutral *uh* sound provides the most resonance of all vowels and should serve as a home base for all sounds we make.
- The primary function of the nasal cavity is to produce sounds like *mm*, *nn*, and *ng*, as well as certain vowels in

French. Some nasal resonance is necessary for producing a healthy sound, however, since slight differences in quality can be detected when a singer is suffering from a cold.

- The term *placement* refers to where the singer feels vibration the most on a particular sound, not to where the sound is actually directed or vibrating within the body.

- The term *dark* refers to a sound that is perhaps too resonant, while the term *bright* may indicate a lack of resonance.

- *Projection*, a quick-fix term used by many directors and musical directors, may indicate that vibrations *within* the body must be increased, thereby increasing vibrations *outside* the body.

- Although it's debatable whether particular resonating chambers have any actual bearing on a sound or not, the singer is able to re-create and manipulate previously successful sounds by remembering their attending sensations.

A Word About Register

While we know a great deal about how the voice works, the subject of vocal register is a bit enigmatic. In the process of studying singing, one is likely to hear the word *register* used in a variety of ways. In simplest of terms, it refers to any particular region of the voice in which a series of tones is produced in a like manner. Tones considered to be in the same register are produced with similar vocal fold posture and resonate in the same part of the body. Positioning the vocal folds to produce a medium-pitch tone full of vitality will create vibrations in the chest, while tones that are higher and less intense—requiring fewer muscles in the vocal mechanism—will tend to vibrate in the head. In this way, the vocal mechanism and the resonating system work dynamically together to create sounds in different registers.

Take, for example, the sound produced by a man in everyday speaking. It is generally low in pitch and somewhat robust in quality. When a man mimics a woman in a comedic manner, he raises the pitch of his voice and allows it to "flip" to a higher register that resonates in the head, in particular, the *falsetto* register. Women can create the same effect by switching to their upper register, though the difference in sound is not as marked. The same effect is achieved by singers who yodel. This style of singing is created by rapidly switching back and forth between lower and upper registers.

Both men and women have three useful vocal registers. There is a low, vibrant *chest voice*, where most of our everyday speaking occurs, a *mixed voice* that is higher in pitch and less substantial in sound, and a higher *upper register*, or head voice, where the sound seems to resonate in the head. While additional registers do exist, both between and beyond the ones discussed here, they are less pronounced and more subjective than this text can afford to be. In order to discover them, one must first become comfortable with the ones outlined here.

The chest voice is the easiest to find, since much of our everyday speaking occurs in this register. It's called the chest voice because the vocal folds are positioned to create sounds that vibrate in the chest. Almost everyone speaks in chest voice naturally. In musical theatre singing, this part of the voice is often called the "belt" (possibly derived from the fact that singing produced in this register requires more activity in the abdominal region.) For years, classically trained singers have been taught that the chest voice is not a legitimate register for artistic singing. It was—and still is—frequently regarded by some teachers as "Broadway" singing. While this area of the voice is more useful in musical theatre than opera, it is not the only one an actor will use.

Most men sing in the chest voice naturally, so to say that men "belt" is a bit misleading. Similarly, women work to develop a useful upper register, so to say that falsetto exists in women is somewhat inaccurate as well. While both men and women have a mixed register, it is clearly more prominent and useful in the female voice. Women are likely to use all three registers of their voice in musical theatre repertoire, while men may use the chest exclusively. For men, the mixed voice is discovered through extensive training and exploration. It is useful in singing notes that lie in the uppermost part of the range, just before moving into falsetto. The falsetto voice for men is generally used for chorus singing or for a particular vocal effect.

Because the issue of registers in the voice is somewhat subjective, the process of determining someone's vocal "type" is precarious. In musical theatre, we generally divide voices into four classifications: soprano/alto for women and tenor/bass for men. In musical theatre, voices are often quickly classified out of the need for an equal distribution of voice parts in the chorus. However, a singer should *never* equate his placement in a chorus with his voice classification. Being asked to sing alto in an ensemble doesn't necessarily mean you're an alto. The only way a singer can determine the full range of possibilities is with private instruction.

It is because of our tendency to label voices quickly that we have women who think they are tenors or basses. This is *not* possible. The four classifications designate the differences between male and female voices irrespective of pitches that can or cannot be sung. While some women are very comfortable in the lower part of their voice and may be able to sing lower than men in some cases, they cannot call themselves tenor or bass. It's like calling an unripened tomato an apple simply because it is green.

In most cases, women who think they have unusually low voices have simply not discovered an upper register, no matter how convinced they may be that it doesn't exist. Many women come to me for the first time and say, "I'm an alto." They want to make this perfectly clear from the beginning, hoping that I won't ask them to sing in their upper register. Upon exploring the voice, however, we almost always discover a useful upper register. This doesn't mean that a tone worthy of performance is readily available, however. Areas of the voice that are underused are underdeveloped. The only way to make use of them is through regular exercise. Like any kind of muscular development in the body, the vocal mechanism must be trained to respond in certain ways. This process takes time.

Most of the women actors I teach are between the ages of nineteen and twenty-four. Many of them enter our program having never explored their upper register, if they've explored a singing voice at all. There is always fear and trepidation when I assign a song that requires them to visit this part of their voice. This fear can be so intense that some students will burst into tears in front of the class when they first perform it. While it's my hope that this doesn't need to happen, it is often necessary. Such an emotional response is not always because there's some sort of pain somewhere—many times it's due to the fear or excitement that emanates from sharing a part of oneself that has previously been dormant. If some sort of emotional release will later lead to discovery, it's worth it.

After pursuing vocal study for a short time, most women discover they have a soprano voice and most men a baritone, a medium voice between bass and tenor. True altos and tenors are much less common, which is why most leading roles in musicals are for sopranos and baritones. There are other vocal types—contralto, mezzo soprano, lyric soprano, and coloratura in the female voice, for example—that can be determined only by a professional teacher through private study.

In short, exploring the various registers of the voice can be helpful in determining what type of roles you can play, but singers must guard against being labeled too quickly, especially in a business where jobs are difficult get. You should be no more quick to put "alto" on your resume than you would "character actor." The goal is to be transformable, not limited.

▪ ▪ ▪ 9 ▪ Articulation:
The Coordinator

Once a sound has been modified by resonating chambers, it passes through a particular coordination of muscles to become a specific sound. This final phase is called *articulation*. Articulators include but are not limited to the teeth, lips, tongue, hard palate, and soft palate. Articulators coordinate all aspects of singing, from the point of activating the breath to allowing a sound to resonate and be released.

There is a wealth of terminology used to describe this process, so perhaps a bit of clarification is warranted: to *articulate* or *enunciate* (used interchangeably) means to pronounce words clearly, to the point of being understood. *Pronunciation* is an aspect of articulation, referring to an accepted standard of correctness. *Diction* is the manner in which articulation is achieved—the way in which specific vowels and consonants are produced.

The two basic sounds involved in articulation are consonants and vowels. The difference between the two is how they are produced: A vowel is essentially any sound that can be made without resistance from the teeth, tongue, or lips. It is also the nucleus of a syllable and can always be sustained. A consonant is defined by the manner in which the teeth, tongue, or lips modify and create or interrupt the sound. Consonants also define the borders of syllables and are less resonant than vowels. Understanding how vowels and consonants are shaped not only aids the singer in clarity of communication but can also change the tone and improve the quality of sound. In this way, resonance and articulation are dynamically connected.

Consonants

Consonants are generally divided into two categories: *voiced* and *unvoiced,* or *voiceless*. The primary difference between them is that voiced sounds have pitch, whether spoken or sung; unvoiced sounds do not.

There is a series of consonants that can be paired together as voiced and unvoiced. The letters *b* and *p* are one such pair. Place your hand on your chest and make a *b* sound several times in a row. Notice the vibrations that are present. Now make a *p* sound several times and notice the absence of vibration. Another way to observe the difference is to plug up your ears and alternate between the two; *b* will be much louder than *p*. The reason these two consonants are paired together is that they are produced by the same articulation process: with teeth apart, lips closed, and air being forced between them. The difference is that the vocal folds are active for *b* and inactive for *p*.

The same is true for the sounds typically produced by the letters *d* and *t*. Notice how the tongue touches the roof of the mouth in exactly the same way for both; speak the words *dime* and *time* to illustrate. Similar observations can be made in the case of *j* and *ch* as in *junk* and *chunk*. For *g* as in *goat* and *k* as in *coat*, the back of the tongue moves upward to touch the roof of the mouth. Notice how the teeth and lips work together to produce *v* and *f* as in *veer* and *fear* in a similar way.

Other examples include *w* and *wh* as in *way* and *whey*; voiced and unvoiced *th* as in *than* and *thing*; *z* and *s* as in *zoo* and *sue*; and *zh* and *sh* as in *measure* and *unsure*. In each case, there is a voiced and unvoiced sound articulated in exactly the same way. Except for *h*, all other consonant sounds in speaking and singing are voiced.

Consonants can also be placed in three different movement categories: *continuants, plosives* and *glides*. Continuant sounds are sustained on the breath and include *f, h, l, m, n, ng, r, s, v* and *z*—note that some are voiced, others are unvoiced. All vowel sounds must be considered continuants as well, since they are produced on the breath and can be sustained indefinitely. Plosive consonants are those that stop the breath in order to be produced, including *b, p, d, t, g,* and *k*.

Glides function somewhat as both consonants and vowels in that they begin with a vowel sound but function as a consonant, such as *y* in the word *you*. Pronounce this word very slowly and notice that in actuality it begins with an *ee* sound just before it moves into what we think of as *y*. The same is true for the word *will*. Pronounce it very slowly and notice how it begins with an *oo* sound. The *wh* sound at the beginning of a word is actually a combination of three vowel and consonant sounds: *h, oo,* and *w,* all of which occur before the vowel sound that follows (*when, what,* and *where* are all examples).[1] There is an additional, less common, type of glide used at the beginning of words like *human* and *huge*. This sound is actually created by the sounds *h, ee,* and *y,* all of which take place before the *oo* vowel that follows. In any case, a glide is just that: a glide. Singers should understand how such sounds are formed but must be careful not to overstate them. Attempts to elongate glides result in annoying overcorrection that's sure to point out exactly how little one knows about diction.

A *fricative* consonant is one produced by some sort of friction that limits the amount of breath released, such as the teeth against the lower lip for the *f* and *v* sounds or the teeth coming close together for the *s* and *z* sounds. The *h* sound is also considered fricative because of the narrow opening in the throat that creates friction with the breath. There are several other classifications of consonants, such as *nasals* (*n, m, ng*), *aspirates* (*h, wh, th*), and *affricates* (*j* and *ch*), that lie beyond the scope of this text.

Consonants are both helpful and problematic for the singer. It's important to sing voiced consonants whenever possible in order to be clearly understood. While voiced continuants shouldn't be sustained for any real length of time, a singer should be aware of their capacity for pitch. Likewise, consonants that stop the flow of breath can impede the quality of sound if the singer overenunciates.

---

1. It should be noted that there are regions of the United States that pronounce these words with a voiced *w* as in *want*.

Vowels

Because they are sustained, vowel sounds determine the vocal tone of a singer. Because vowels can be changed by the posture of resonating chambers, they are as much a function of resonance as articulation. In fact, some studies of the voice speak only of consonants with regard to articulation and discuss vowel sounds as an actual part of the resonation process.

Regardless of how they're viewed, vowels are directly influenced by two of the primary articulators: the tongue and lips. While it's possible to make some vowel sounds without significant involvement of the tongue, it is essential that the tongue be allowed to move as necessary when changing from one vowel to another. The lips are especially helpful in determining the difference among some vowels, as outlined below.

Vowels are generally classified as *front, back,* and *central,* depending on the position of the tongue for each. In the case of the vowels *ee, ih, ay, eh,* and *a* (as in *cat),* the front of the tongue (the area just behind the tip) is in the highest position. Notice how the highest point moves slightly backward from one vowel to the next. In the case of the vowels *ah, aw, oh, oo* (as in *foot),* and *oo* (as in *flute),* the highest part of the tongue is in the very back. While the lips are of little use in the front vowels, they are essential in differentiating among the back vowels—notice how they are increasingly closed when the back vowels are pronounced in the order above. The primary central vowels include *uh* and the various forms of *er,* depending on the amount of *r* sound present. Here the highest point of the tongue is in the middle.

To clearly differentiate between tongue positions, say the vowels *ee, uh, oh* in succession. Notice the dramatic changes in tongue position between each: for *ee,* it feels as though the tongue is touching the roof of the mouth; for *uh,* the tongue seems flat and relaxed; for *oh,* the tongue seems pulled downward slightly. The *tip* of the tongue should reside comfortably behind the teeth for all vowel sounds.

Singers are often required to modify vowel sounds in order to achieve maximum resonance, especially in the upper register. For example, the *ee* vowel, perhaps the most difficult to sing in the upper chest voice, is often modified toward *ih*. This enables the singer to find more resonance and prevents the voice from cracking. Similarly, *oo* as in *flute* may be modified to *oo* as in *foot*; *ay* to *eh*; *ah* to *uh* and so forth. In short, front and back vowels tend to merge toward central vowels in the upper register. Many singers who insist on singing pure vowels in the upper register put undue strain on the voice. In contrast, singers who tend to overmodify in the upper register are less likely to be understood. A balance between clarity and healthy singing must be achieved.

When two or more vowels appear consecutively in the same syllable, a diphthong is created. In the word *light*, for example, the central vowel sound is actually *ah* followed by *ih*, though slight differences in *ih* occur among dialects and regions. Pronounce it slowly: *lah-iht*. In normal speech, the first sound, *ah*, is sustained longer than the second sound, *ih*. Other diphthong examples include the primary vowel sounds in the words *plate* (*eh* followed by *ee* to produce *ay*); *now* (*ah* followed by *oo* as in *foot*); *no* (*oh* followed by *oo* as in *foot*); and *toy* (the short *oh* followed by *ih*). As with a glide, the singer must be careful not to overarticulate a diphthong. If the singer gives too much attention to the final vowel sound, the word becomes distorted.

Merging Consonants and Vowels

To get a better feel for how consonants and vowels work together, try singing any simple song with vowels only, no consonants. You'll notice two important things: (1) the words are unintelligible without consonants, and (2) you may not know exactly how to produce many of the vowels. This is because consonants have considerable influence over vowel production, and to suddenly remove them from the process of communication means vowels may become distorted. It behooves the singer, however, to be aware of subtle adjustments in vowel production that enable him to find more resonance and freedom in the voice. Remember, we're talking about technique that you should forget in performance.

THE LIPS

The lips are used to shape the sound externally and should never be held in a tight position. The tendency to pull them back in the lower register and/or downward in the upper register leads to undue tension. Many singers have a tendency to raise their upper lip in a snarling smile to help brighten the tone. Ask yourself: do I want to be snarling when I sing? This technique is neither helpful nor appealing to watch. Similarly, some singers tend to pull the upper lip downward when singing very high tones. This action will mask the sound and darken the tone considerably. It also makes it more difficult to sing certain vowels. Don't overcompensate.

In short, the lips should be no more active in singing than in speaking. Nonetheless, it is common to find singers manipulating tone quality by adjusting the position of the lips. Remember that tone and resonance are uniquely connected, and while lips can adjust the quality of the back vowels, they do little to enhance resonance or tone. The problem of tension in the lips can be addressed by making "motorboat" sounds similar to that of a horse, which will allow the lips to completely relax.

THE LOWER JAW

The muscles in the jaw are often problematic for singers as well. Jaw tension is extremely common in those who are struggling with the emotional challenges of singing. Think about it: what happens in the muscles of the lower jaw when our emotions are running rampant? It's no wonder that nervous singers try to sing through clenched muscles.

In addition to clenching the jaw, there may be a tendency to extend it downward and outward when singing higher notes. Try doing this intentionally several times and you'll notice how much effort it takes to hold it in position. Nonetheless, fear, anxiety, and emotional issues—or simply habit—will force the jaw into this position without the singer even knowing it. Many will wonder why their jaw muscles are sore after they've been singing for a while.

The lips must also be relaxed in order for the jaw to open freely. On higher pitches in the upper register, the jaw must be allowed to drop to its maximum opening (again, not forced downward). Singing higher tones requires more resonance in the voice, especially in the oral cavity. If the jaw is too closed or too open, resonance will be impeded and the sound fraught with tension.

A few exercises that will help loosen a tight jaw include moving it from side to side and saying *yah, yah, yah* several times, releasing any tension that may be present. You can also imagine you are in a sleeping position, where the jaw naturally drops open. While you cannot always keep the jaw in this position, it should feel that it can go there at any time without being forced.

THE TONGUE

The tongue is without a doubt the most important of the articulators because it is the most mobile. The number of positions to which the tongue can adjust is uncountable. With its flexibility comes potential tension as well. Like the jaw, the tongue needs a "home base" to return to until it is required to do something else. This position should be flat in the mouth, not pointed, curved, forced down, or flexed in any way, with the tip resting behind the lower teeth. It is most likely the position your tongue is in while you're reading this now. The tip of the tongue should never leave this position for vowel sounds, only for consonants. Remember that the front, middle, and back areas of the tongue are raised for their respective vowels, but the tip should always remain forward, resting comfortably behind the teeth.

Even for consonants, the tongue should never be pulled back in the throat. Although it's true that for some vowels, especially *ee*, the tongue is required to do a moderate amount of work, a singer should guard against making too much of it, lest effort become tension. If the tongue is fraught with tension, then it is not able to move freely to do its work; therefore, any movement in the tongue must be quick, precise, and free.

Consonants appear in one of three places in a word: the beginning, middle, or end. Many teachers tell their students to overenunciate consonants so they are clearly understood. This is logical because consonants do not have the same resonant qualities as vowel sounds. Many directors and musical directors will ask, especially when working with an ensemble of singers, for "more final consonants." Being understood is the responsibility of the singer, and an extremely important one at that, but, as illustrated in the next section, this idea can be carried to an extreme. A singer should remember that *all* consonants must be sung when possible, not just the final ones. Even those that are not voiced should be allowed to "ride the breath" whenever possible to ensure that communication is taking place.

Coordinating the body to make a sung sound is the responsibility of the articulators. The time it takes for all elements of singing to coordinate is only a matter of a moment. The articulators will often shape a sound while the breath is entering the body. There is an indelible connection between the impulse for a sound and what physically happens to produce it. While the process can be traced methodically, it's as if impulse and sound are one and the same.

Summary of Articulation

- Articulators include the teeth, lips, tongue, hard palate, and soft palate, and they shape a sound into a specific word or syllable.
- Articulators also serve as coordinators for the entire singing process.
- Vowel sounds are made without resistance from the teeth, tongue, or lips. Consonants are modified by them.
- There are two general types of consonants: *voiced* and *unvoiced*. Voiced consonants require vocal cord approximation; unvoiced do not.
- All vowels are voiced when sung, though they can be whispered when spoken.
- There are three types of vowel sounds, classified by the highest position of the tongue: *front, back,* and *central*.

- Other forms of modification are dependent upon the register in which a vowel is sung.
  - Vowels sung in the upper register are often modified to a more open sound, allowing greater resonance.
- The lips, lower jaw, and tongue work dynamically together to merge consonants and vowels into specific sounds.
- In general, solid vocal technique must be practiced religiously. In performance, the actor learns to trust that his technique will automatically serve him.

Resonance and Articulation in Performance

While resonance and diction are of profound importance in singing and acting, our obsession with them leads to many pitfalls. Preoccupation with diction is rampant among singers. It's true that singing alters the rhythm of an otherwise spoken text, calling attention to sounds that might otherwise go unnoticed. Yet, many singers perceive diction as an inherent "problem" in singing. Their solution: "articulate more." I'm not even sure what that means. Articulation is not all there is to communicating. One can speak with utmost clarity, but if there's no personal awareness of what's being said, if there's no emotional attachment, then it is meaningless.

Once he has mastered the mechanics of diction, an actor who is present in the moment, connected to his text, and willing to share his emotions freely will invariably communicate— whether speaking or singing. This is not to say that clarity is unimportant, it is paramount. But clarity is a function of the *soul*, not the body. If energy is transferred from the acting process to the vocal process, then one's technique is suddenly revealed. Overenunciation and "projecting," like programmed gestures, will not, under any circumstance, compensate for bad acting.

The true remedy for these issues can be found in one's emotional availability: the actor/singer who is well-versed in technique and willing to share his emotions more generously will find that both clarity and volume are nonissues. Singing is a form of acting. Whenever the acting suffers, so will the singing.

Because directors, musical directors, and voice teachers often command "more of this" or "more of that," actor/singers fall prey to such unhealthy practices. However, it is the performer's responsibility to interpret direction. Remember that not all directors are versed in acting technique, and some teachers of voice don't address the issue of acting at all. We can spend lots of energy hoping for the day when a common language is established, but in the meantime we must find practical solutions that do not interfere with our goal: to communicate truthfully.

A Final Word on Technique

Much of the technical discussion in this book has focused on all the things that cause a voice to malfunction. The fact remains that once we let go of all that stands in our way, singing is remarkably simple. A singer must work very hard at not working very hard.

Solid vocal technique is crucial to developing a healthy singing voice, but it simply will not work if it is all a performer thinks about in performance. I cannot overstate the fact that technique must be learned in the studio and promptly forgotten on the stage. Singing is not just about the voice, nor is it just about acting. It is a delicate balance of both. Each must be addressed separately at times but never exclusively.

III

Applying Your Voice

*"The joy of standing on a mountain top
and the joy of the ascent are indivisible."*

—Alfred Harbage

...■10■ Finding a Teacher

As stated earlier, no one can really learn to sing from a book. Learning techniques of healthy vocal production requires consistent monitoring by a mentor. For most singers there is one such type: the voice teacher. Finding the right teacher is a challenge, and many actors waste time and money on the search because they don't know what to look for.

Voice teachers are experienced singers who have studied voice and how to teach it, enabling them to diagnose and correct technical issues in the voice. Voice teachers are often responsible for developing a singer's artistry and musical expression as well, especially in the early stages of study. Once a singer has mastered the basics—usually after a number of years—he or she may seek out a vocal coach. Vocal coaches are employed strictly to develop musical expression, interpretation, and diction. They usually do not coach singers in vocal technique. Most vocal coaches are accomplished pianists or conductors who have mastered performance styles of opera or musical theatre.

Many voice teachers who offer training in musical theatre have had significant training in opera as well. The basics of healthy singing are inherent in this repertoire, and it can't be sung without proper training. An actor who pursues vocal study should always look for this background in a voice teacher and expect to sing some of the repertoire. Classical vocal training does for the singer what Shakespeare does for the modern actor; a knowledge of the classics is essential for success in contemporary styles. There are instances in which companies will even call for an operatic aria at an audition, especially for shows like *A Little Night Music, Phantom of the Opera*, or *Master Class.*

Many college-level teachers who specialize in opera and art

song[1] technique do not allow students to sing musical theatre songs until they have mastered the basics of singing. Because many musical theatre songs are easy to learn, they can be sung with poor technique, especially in the beginning stages of study. Some teachers will discourage a singer from musical theatre altogether, claiming that it will destroy the voice. Such teachers tend to stereotype all musical theatre singers as belters who "grind out" the sound without regard for vocal technique. While this may be true for some actors, it's unfair to say that musical theatre is destructive to the voice. If sung poorly, any type of music—especially opera—will damage the voice. Fortunately, many qualified teachers support an interest in musical theatre as long as students are willing to sing it well.

What to Avoid

In the paragraphs that follow, I outline some approaches that an actor first learning to sing will want to avoid. It may be unfair to say that all such approaches are invalid, but there is clear reason for caution in each case. While a variety of singing methods are equally justifiable, there are extremists that do more harm than good.

As evidenced in this book, a good voice teacher understands and employs principles of scientific vocal technique. It's important to be able to diagnose and correct vocal issues with proven solutions. However, many teachers carry this method to an extreme. Recent scientific developments in the field of vocal anatomy have provided us with a clearer understanding of how the voice works—no longer are we subject to the mystique of the past. It only makes sense that with this new information comes a vigorous enthusiasm for teaching it. It's truly exciting to be able to talk about the voice in ways that we were not able to twenty years ago, but we must not be overindulgent. The teacher who analyzes every tone a student makes is in danger of creating a Frankensteinian creature void of expression, depth, and honesty. Remember that while a pleasant, healthy sound is desir-

---

1. Art songs are classical poems set to music and make up the bulk of repertoire heard in college voice recitals.

able, a singer who cannot communicate has failed to sing. You should only study with such a teacher if you are confident that the technique learned will not override your artistry.

In contrast, teachers who speak only of artistry and communication are endangering the vocal health of their students by ignoring important principles of how the voice works. Many such teachers speak in terms of imagery only, providing little help with actual technique. Since many muscles of the voice seem to work involuntarily, we must manipulate them by means of imagery or sensation. Asking a student to imagine the sound is coming out the top of his head is helpful only if the student has created that image himself. Productive vocal study is the result of developing a common language between student and teacher. It cannot take place when a student is forced to re-create sensations felt by someone else. A teacher who speaks only in mystifying terminology will build a voice destined for trouble. He may offer good advice in the way of artistry and interpretation but may not possess the technical vocabulary needed to build solid technique. You should only study with such a teacher if you know your technique is firmly in place. If this is the case, a vocal coach is probably a better choice anyway.

Many intelligent teachers find themselves caught in a "one solution fits all" trap. Such teachers only talk about the voice in relation to single concepts such as "vowel placement," "breath," "resonance," "agility," or "diction," claiming that all vocal problems are directly related to one of these issues. Teachers who follow a pattern like this have typically done so for years, and most have done no recent study or reading on the subject they teach. A single-solution teacher may also believe that what worked for him as a student of singing will work for everyone. But every voice is unique, as is every relationship between teacher and student. So when a friend says that he's made great strides with a particular teacher, don't assume the same will be true for you. It could be that a student's particular needs happen to be met by a teacher's strength or approach. A teacher who uses a "single-solution" method may lack essential training, necessary teaching skills, or ambition for personal growth. Talk with a number of students in a studio and compare their experiences, looking for a variety of success stories.

The tendency to quickly classify a voice can also be a problem. As stated in Chapter 8, this is most precarious territory, especially in theatre. Remember that a qualified teacher will take ample time to determine your vocal type. Likewise, you should never attempt to pressure a teacher into a premature decision about your voice type.

What to Look For

The ideal teacher is perhaps impossible to define and must always be regarded as ideal. Such a teacher will strive for a balance between the extremes and cultivate principles of stability and personal growth. She will also maintain an organized body of information, a willingness to compare it to new ideas, and the ability to develop solid musicianship in every student.

You should look for a teacher who can speak in technical terms but who also understands what it means to communicate. A qualified teacher does not follow the same exact regimen for each student and does not teach exactly the same way today as he did thirty-five years ago. Many teachers are afraid of new information that requires them to rethink traditional practice. But a sound teacher is open to changes that support or reflect his or her particular philosophy.

Balanced teachers are generally modest in nature and are less likely to parade their technique about the land. No one can claim that singing will be learned only in his or her studio, and qualified teachers will be the first to admit they don't know all there is know about the voice. No one does.

A teacher's track record is also important, but it should not be the defining factor. Some teachers continually produce successful students, while others do not. It's possible for a below-average teacher to take credit for a singer who's been very successful—in spite of the fact that the singer may have gone on to study with someone else.

Finally, *don't* judge the quality of a teacher by his singing voice alone. There are many teachers with great voices who do not fully understand what it is they do. Their teaching methods often include superimposing their own concepts onto other singers whose voices are completely different. A great singer does not a great teacher make. In contrast, a teacher who doesn't "wow" you with a lovely voice may very well be excellent in the studio. The best teacher I've ever known experienced many technical problems in singing that she was not able to remedy until many years into her career. While retraining her voice led to wonderful singing, the quality (by her own admission) was not what it would have been had she learned to sing correctly in the first place. Because she had worked through so many issues in her own singing, however, she was a fabulous teacher. Recall the carpenter who builds from talent and the one who creates from skills he has learned: whose platform would you rather stand on?

Where to Start

You can begin the search for the right teacher by contacting the music department at a local college or university. Most departments offer a course called Class Voice, designed to introduce you to the basic skills of singing. If you're ready for one-on-one instruction, begin by asking for bios on college voice faculty, or find them in programs or school catalogs. Attend recitals presented by students and make some assessments of your own. It's always good to get to know a few students of a particular teacher before you begin to study with him or her. This gives you a better idea of what you can expect and what will be expected of you.

Next, set up an introductory meeting or first lesson with a teacher. This is where you will get the most valuable information. Ask questions, share your experiences, and outline your goals and what you hope to achieve. It's also important to assess what you're ready for versus what you're going to get from a teacher. Will the instructor explain the ideas and concepts in a way that makes sense to you or will the instruction be over your head?

Determine if there are any professional organizations to which a teacher belongs. The National Association of Teachers of

Singing (NATS) is perhaps the most prestigious and in recent years has embraced musical theatre as a viable category of its competitions. Membership in organizations such as Music Educator's National Conference (MENC) or other nationally recognized groups is often a good sign. Unfortunately, there is no professional standard that a voice teacher must meet in order to declare himself an expert. Anyone can hang a sign on a door and set up a lucrative business for teaching voice.

Once you find a teacher, there is always the question of cost. Finding a qualified teacher at a nominal rate is not as difficult as it might seem. I personally know of teachers in metropolitan areas who charge more than one hundred dollars for an hour of instruction. Such teachers usually work with professional actors and singers on a regular basis. Some of them offer a product worthy of this fee, some do not. In reality, there are voice teachers throughout the country who offer quality instruction at an affordable rate—especially for a beginner.

I hope these observations don't make you suspicious of every teacher you may encounter. My goal is to break down some of the misconceptions about teachers and what makes them successful, not to frighten away potential students. There are many qualified teachers who deserve to have the best students. You want to be one of those students.

Remember, it's *your money* and *your voice*, so be selective.

• • • 11 • Your First Song

As a beginning singer, it's important that you enjoy success in choosing and preparing your first song, whether for a class, audition, or an actual performance. Singing is not a form of everyday communication, so when faced with performing a song, there's no real-life experience from which we can draw. However, there are songs with lyrics that speak of situations that we might have experienced. Such songs give us a personal perspective and enable us to offer more truthful performances. Like acting, we must be comfortable singing as ourselves before we can create characters who sing.

Finding a Song

If you don't know where to begin to look for a song, visit a local college library or a music store that sells musical theatre scores. Look for a variety of collections, anthologies, and full scores of musical plays. I strongly suggest the beginning singer choose a song from early musical theatre (pre-1950). Songs by Richard Rodgers and Lorenz Hart, Jerome Kern, or Irving Berlin are always good choices. Many of these songs can be taken out of context and can stand alone as audition material as well.

Once you find a collection or anthology, begin to peruse lyrics, song by song, looking for ideas or sentiments that reflect a personal experience. Always consider songs that have "I" in the title or the main body of the song. Such songs generally tell the listener who you are and how you relate to another individual or situation. This is why lyrics about romance, whether serious or comical, are often the best audition songs. Avoid soliloquies or character songs (songs that must be sung by a particular character in a particular play in order for the lyric to make sense). Focus on songs that enable you to sing directly to another person.

Since many song lyrics are poetic in nature, some of them use poetic language that may not be part of your everyday vocabulary. In early musical theatre you may find words and/or colloquialisms you've never heard. Don't be too quick to discount a lyric in such cases. Just because it contains words or phrases that you may not use in a real conversation doesn't mean you can't be convincing when you sing them. Look at the story of the song and ask if you can relate to it in any way.

Make a list of possible song choices based on your observations. Don't just ask yourself if you like the song; determine if it's one you can communicate effectively. Picking a song just because it appeals to them is perhaps the most common mistake actors make in choosing material. Remaining open to material that doesn't reach out and grab you right away often leads to wonderful discoveries.

After you find a few options, you'll want to determine which songs lie in your comfortable singing range. No one should ever risk an audition by singing a song that is outside his range. The voice can be unpredictable under pressure, and auditions are too important. If you can't determine whether a song is in your range, then you must get with a pianist.

If you think about it long enough, you probably know someone in this business who reads music and plays piano.[1] Spend a few minutes singing scales with your piano player and have him determine what your comfortable range is. Once you've done so, ask him to look at your selected song possibilities and determine which ones are appropriate for you. If none of them lie in your range, have the pianist show you where your range is on the musical staff so that you can begin to judge for yourself. It's a good idea to be able to state what your singing range is anyway, so commit this information to memory, with the understanding that studying with a qualified teacher can change it.

---

1. Unless this person is a really good friend, don't ask him to help you without first offering to pay him. If it's your best friend, buy him dinner at the very least.

How Goes the Song?

Once you've found a song that suits your personality and voice, you can begin your work. Understand that *learning* a song is different from *performing* a song. Learning the song involves processing and internalizing the mechanics of it: exactly what notes to sing and how long to hold them. Performing a song means laying the mechanics aside and conveying the lyric. Many singers feel they are ready to perform a song once they have learned it, but this is not likely to be the case. Important work on effectively communicating a lyric is required before any sharing can be done. This doesn't mean that you have to find deep meaning in everything—most musical theatre songs are very straightforward in what they have to say—but you must understand every word of your lyric.

A simple awareness of how to sing the song as though it has never been sung before is often the key. In the case of a monologue, we give ourselves permission to find spontaneity, to live in the moment and to make discoveries. The same should be true for a song. But in singing, notes and rhythms are prescribed for us, limiting our spontaneity. The successful singer is the one who treats his song as monologue first and through a gradual process, expands his speech into full-fledged singing.

The guidelines below will take you on this journey in a practical, systematic manner. This approach is not the only valid one, however. Remember that we all process and learn differently. Take from it what makes sense to you and make it your own.

THE LYRIC

The most important element of your song is the lyric. Understand *exactly* what the lyric means. Countless is the number of times I have witnessed an actor in an audition or performance who has no idea what he's singing about. Such a performer is too quick to rely on the song and the sound of his voice to do the work.

Singing is like Shakespeare: it's possible to deliver the material, sound good, and have no idea what you're saying.

There's common tendency to "play the emotion" of the song, saying that a lyric is simply "pensive," "reflective," or "joyous." This is like saying Macbeth is simply a murderer. These qualifiers do not give us enough information. You must know what every word, every nuance, every moment is about, and you must live in it.

Perhaps the best example to illustrate this point is Sondheim's "Send in the Clowns," which you should *never* sing at an audition unless asked. Many people hear a powerful song like this and immediately add it to their audition material, without regard for what the lyric really means. People hear it and think, "Oh, wow, that's a really sad song. My voice will sound really good singing that." The actor paying attention to the lyric, however, realizes that this song can't be taken out of context. In order to sing this song, you *must* be a fifty-year-old actress who regrets the fact that she didn't pursue a relationship years ago that, under different circumstances, would be available to her now. Understanding that the song is "emotional" does nothing for you as a performer until you've explored the text yourself.

If you have a lyric in front of you that can't stand on its own, choose something else. You will do more specific work on your lyric later in the exercise, but for now, have a clear understanding of what you will be communicating. Do this by speaking the lyric out loud several times, listening intently to what it is saying.

THE MELODY

The next step is to become familiar with the melody, which is essentially "how the song goes." To demonstrate what the melody is, choose a nursery rhyme or folk song and hum it. Notice that there are two basic elements of what you do: the notes (ranging from low to high) and the rhythm (the relationship between how long notes are held—some longer or shorter than others). The melody is composed of words, notes, and rhythmic patterns and is the part that you will sing.

All other components of the song constitute the *accompaniment*. The accompaniment is played on the piano or by an orchestra in a production. Notes and rhythms used in the accompaniment may be similar or different from those found in the melody. This is why it's important to be secure in the mechanics of the melody before singing with accompaniment. Once the two are combined, you'll discover how your notes fit into the accompaniment.

The process of learning notes and rhythms is enigmatic. Different singers learn in different ways. For many beginners, hearing another person sing the song is helpful. While you have your pianist available, have her record herself playing and/or singing the melody of your song on a tape for you, perhaps slightly slower than the performance tempo. This will give you the technical information you need.

Avoid acting your song until the words, rhythm, and melody are clearly formed in your mind. This is tricky, especially for someone whose expertise is acting, but it's important to not make choices too early in the learning process. Once you have learned the song, there are specific steps I recommend for creating a truthful performance. If you're learning to sing for the first time, you will be most comfortable relying on communication skills you've mastered as an actor. The steps I outline will work with any technique with which you are comfortable, so be ready to apply any and all of your acting tools to your song.

A Lesson with Stuart: Getting Real

Recently a professional actor, Stuart, approached me for help with his singing. His training had been primarily in opera and art song, yet most of his professional work had been in nonmusical theatre. When we met, he explained that he wanted help finding the style of musical theatre to which his voice was most suited. Already knowing Stuart and his training, I suspected that "classical" musical theatre would come very easy for him and that more contemporary styles might require some shaping. I explained that with his training he was capable of most anything—that it would be a matter of transforming his voice into a particular style, whether it be Rodgers and Hammerstein, Sondheim, or pop/rock.

Stuart had prepared a couple of songs from different eras of musical theatre. I suggested a more contemporary song and had him sing it a couple of times. As he did, I observed a lovely vocal quality that was rich and full. His pitch was centered, his diction perfect, and he was singing long, full phrases. In spite of all the wonderful sounds he made, I wasn't interested in what he had to say—it was all about his technique. Stuart had put on his habitual "musical theatre" face, thinking he was acting the song. But it was clear that he was focused on technique and simply "playing" the emotion.

When we were finished, I asked him, "How do you feel about what you just did?"

"It was okay," he said. "I think I tend to connect phrases together when I probably should breathe more frequently. My opera training has taught me to do that. In general, I think I'm working too hard."

The symptom he described was on track; however, the solution was not. Simply choosing additional places to breathe or phrase wasn't going to make his singing any more interesting. I began to suspect that Stuart was not uncomfortable with style as much as he was with communication.

I asked, "Who are you singing this song to?"

Silence. The question clearly caught him off-guard. He finally said, "I'm not sure. I hadn't thought about it really."

I knew that if he were living truthfully in the lyric, he wouldn't have to think about where to breathe and explained that the technical problems he observed were really the result of a larger acting issue. I suggested he spend a few moments with the lyric to see if he could make any personal connection to it. I asked him to name someone to whom he might sing this song.

He studied for a few moments and said, "Well, I would probably say my wife, but we're not really at this particular place, so I'm not sure."

"That's okay, you don't have to have a final answer yet. In theatre, you will either be singing to someone else or to yourself. In this case, it's not yourself, so let's find someone for now. You can always change your mind."

I outlined the importance of doing his homework on a song, much in the same way he would on a monologue. He had to decide whom he was singing to, how long he had known the person, what the circumstances of their relationship were, and what precipitating events had led up to the moment before the song. Sure, he could go to the script of the show for this information, but if he were performing the song out of context, it would be of very little help to him. He had to first make singing a personal experience.

"In order to create any type of character in a musical," I said, "it's important that we learn to sing as ourselves. This can only be done if we can make some sort of personal connection to the text. Sing to your wife for now and we'll see what happens.

"Now, let's look more closely at the lyric. I want you to begin by speaking the text of the song as though it were a monologue, without regard for the written rhythm. Just act the words. Pretend I'm not here if you like."

After a few moments, he began to speak the lyric freely. Immediately he made a deeper connection to the text than he'd been able to do earlier. I could see him discovering what the words were actually saying. This was only the beginning, however. Stuart was still using a rich, full, perfectly executed stage voice.

"Can you do it once more, and say the words to your wife as though she were sitting across from you?"

This time, I saw more of Stuart and less of an actor performing. He was honest, truthful, and vulnerable—it was extremely empowering for him.

I suggested that his training in opera had in some ways overqualified him, causing him to work much harder at sounding good than he needed to. I explained how musical theatre lives somewhere between reality and opera and that a singing actor who is not able to communicate is destined to deliver an uninteresting performance.

"So, how do I do this when I sing?" he asked with a nervous laugh.

"Well, it's a process, not a leap," I cautioned. "You can't expect to jump right into it without some exploration and discovery. Let's break the song down into phrases and work in small increments."

I had him focus on the first phrase of the song by acting it as spoken text. I also asked that he make observations about his acting choices. He did this several times, focusing on how he would speak the words of the first phrase.

"The next step is a little tricky," I told him. "What I'd like you to do is simply act this phrase on pitch. We're going to keep the same rhythmic freedom, the same acting choices, and the same emotional connection as before, just add pitch."

I gave him a starting note on the piano, but I did not play the melody or the accompaniment. Immediately Stuart started singing as he had done before, with a rich, full voice and romantic tone. I asked him how he felt about this.

"Well, I'm not sure I did what you were asking for," he said.

"What do *you* want it to be?" I asked him.

"Well, I want it to be more like my speech, but I can't seem to do that yet."

I encouraged him to be patient with the process.

"Go back and speak the phrase and then immediately sing it and make no difference between the two," I suggested.

After a few more attempts, Stuart was beginning to see what it meant to sing freely and to speak on pitch. I gave him a moment to think about what he'd done then asked, "What do you notice about this?"

"Well, it's more free, more natural. I notice that I'm not thinking about my voice at all, just the text. But I can't actually sing it like this with the piano, can I? This free rhythm is going to put me out of sync."

"We're not there yet," I reminded him, "Once you're comfortable with what I'm asking you to do now, you can begin to expand into the written rhythm. The difference will be that you will have brought your acting choices with you."

After trying it a few more times, I noticed he was still skeptical. I asked him to share his thoughts.

"Well, I'm certainly acting it more naturally, but I'm not sure of how I sound," he maintained. "I'm afraid my voice is not living up to my standards now. I can't seem to listen to my voice and act at the same time."

"You are right! You *can't* actively listen to your voice and communicate at the same time. Nor do you want to."

I asked him if he could think of an example of someone who isn't a particularly strong singer but who communicates well. He suggested someone and we agreed that this person hadn't had a particularly beautiful voice, but his communication was always honest, truthful, and engaging.

"So what you're saying is a compromise must be reached between my singing and acting," he suggested.

"Well, compromise means that something is sacrificed from both," I told him. "Think of this process as acting *and* singing. Allow one action to support the other. What you don't yet realize, Stuart, is that your voice is still beautiful. You will not lose your technique simply because you're not thinking about it. You have strong vocal training that will serve you no matter what you think about."

This led to the discussion of two important words: *expectation* and *trust*. As audience members, we expect certain things from certain shows; directors expect certain skills to be part of an actor's vocabulary; Actor's Equity expects certain standards will be met in the rehearsal and performance process; and so forth. With such high expectations, we are invariably disappointed when they are not met. But the only sanity there exists is in letting go of our expectations and of how things are *supposed* to turn out. The only way to avoid this frustration is to trust ourselves. Stuart said that he wasn't listening to his voice, and that was scary—scary because his expectations weren't met. He needed to know it was okay to trust himself.

Continuing in our process, we added the next phrase in the same fashion. His connection to the text was improving dramatically with each effort. After a few more times, he experienced a revelation:

"I think I'm comfortable as long as what I'm doing can be explained. With this approach, I can't analyze what I'm doing, so I don't know if it's working or not. This is really ironic," he said, chuckling, "because as actors that's exactly what we want: some-thing that works but can't really be analyzed."

"Exactly! Would you agree that you're communicating truthfully?"

"Yes!"

"Then it's working." Stuart smiled and looked back at his music. I continued: "Sure it helps to tell you that I approve of what you're doing, but you have to approve as well, Stuart. You must trust."

I think Stuart and I both learned that day that an actor is responsible for his own fate. If he begins a song with perfect technique, he sets himself up for failure. If he approaches it with no rules, then there are no rules to break, so he is destined to suc-ceed.

Your Turn to Succeed

The above example should give you some insight into the exer-cises described below. You will find that doing this work with a coach will enhance your discoveries. Talk about your experi-ences throughout the process.

> ### *Know* and *Own* the Lyric
> Write down the lyrics of your song on a separate sheet of paper in paragraph form. This will give you a fresh perspective on what the words have to say. Now read the lyric and get a sense of what the emotional foun-dation of the song really is. Take it at face value— determine all information based on what is included in the song itself. Don't go to the script of the show for information; this is only useful when you're trying to create a specific character. Then answer the following questions as completely as possible.
> 1. *Whom am I singing to?* If you don't know whom you're singing to in performance, then no one will care what you have to say. Don't just create some

generic person, actually name someone in your life to whom you would sing this song.

2. *What are the given circumstances of my song?* To make it your own, you must create a scenario that is relevant to something in your own life. *Where am I?* A park, an apartment, a street? *Where is the person I am singing to?* Beside me, across the room, another country? *What has happened earlier today that led up to this event?* An argument, a discovery? Most importantly, *what has happened the moment before I am compelled to sing?* Write down detailed answers for each of these questions.

3. *What are the acting beats of my song? Where does one idea end and another begin? How does each idea in the lyric reflect my set of given circumstances?* Whatever process you might use to score a monologue can be used here. Flesh out the song and know where you are when it begins, if and how you are changed by it, and where you are when it ends.

If you have chosen a song that meets the criteria stated earlier, you should have no trouble answering these questions. Next you're ready to get specific about communicating the lyric.

Speaking the Lyric

Speak the lyric out loud, allowing yourself to communicate as spontaneously as you would in a monologue. Do this with no regard for the actual rhythm of the lyric; just speak it freely. Don't allow yourself to get caught up in the rhyming pattern. Just speak the words honestly. Repeat this process many times.

Remember that you're working toward a truthful presentation. Before you would ever sing these words, you must be comfortable saying them. As stated earlier, there may be times when certain words are more poetic than those you would use in everyday life. While you cannot change the words to suit you, you can create a subtext or use substitution.

Notice the natural rhythm of your lyric when spoken. This is the rhythm of everyday communication. It depends on *operative* words to make it effective. Operative words move the action forward; they carry the weight of what we're trying to say and are always stressed.

Lyrics of a song are forced into a specific rhythm, however, causing operative words to be lost unless the singer is conscious of them. A good composer tries to reflect the scansion of the spoken text in his music, but we cannot depend on him to do the work for us. *Songs do not sing themselves.*

We must highlight and stress operative words in singing just as we would in speaking. Doing this means getting a little messy. Many actors treat songs as frail works of art that will crumble if we veer the slightest from what's written on the page. In musical theatre, it is expected that you will take certain liberties as long as they are supported by acting choices. This doesn't mean you can change the notes or lyrics to something else, but you can stretch and bend them substantially. Color outside the lines!

With an awareness of operative words in your lyric, continue.

Singing Notes in a Free Rhythm

Speak the first phrase of your song a couple of times as you did before. Notice the rhythm you naturally use. Which syllables are longer or more important or have more weight? Which are less important and are likely to be said very quickly? How does the rhythm of your speech differ from or resemble the rhythm of the song? Using this natural spoken rhythm, speak the phrase again, simply adding notes. You may want to get your starting note from your tape or from a piano. While it will be clear that you are singing, you will still sound like you're speaking because the rhythm is free and natural.

This exercise takes time to master, and it's important to take small steps and work phrase by phrase. Have a teacher or pianist work with you and monitor your progress. Above all, *act* the lyric. If you are always acting, you are doing it right.

The next step is to expand the rhythm. Ballads generally require more expansion than fast-paced songs, which tend to replicate our speech more accurately. Expanding into the written rhythm means expanding your acting as well. In slow ballads, moments become seconds and seconds become minutes. An actor must be willing to expand every moment without "checking out."

Expanding the Rhythm

Speak-sing the first phrase in a free rhythm as before. If you're song is relatively slow in tempo, linger on operative words in the phrase, gradually building them to their full value. Be careful not to rush this process. Sing the phrase several times until what you're doing begins to resemble the written rhythm. Remember to bring your acting choices with you each time.

Work several phrases, if not the entire song, using these exercises. After a while, you'll be ready to sing your song with the accompaniment. You may discover that it's not necessary to work phrase by phrase each time you learn a new song. As your experience increases, so will your natural ability.

The process of performing a song requires three things from the performer: (1) understanding how music works (melody and rhythm), (2) the ability to use one's voice in a free and healthy manner, and (3) skills for acting and singing simultaneously. However, the finished product must never appear to be manufactured of these elements. Technique and artistry must be synthesized into one fluid method. If you are a committed participant in the act of singing, with a desire to say something passionately, you will succeed. It's a matter of trusting yourself to deliver the goods.

...12.Your First Singing Audition

Presenting a song at an audition for the first time can be a bit scary, especially if you're not sure how to prepare. In many cases, an untrained singer with good audition skills will prevail over a fabulous singer who doesn't understand the process. Like many aspects of our business, auditioning is a skill that can be learned. While there are no written rules regarding the audition process, there is an accepted standard for presenting yourself as a singer.

Let's look at an example: A young man, Steve, who has a lovely baritone voice and substantial experience, is auditioning for a character role in a musical, one which doesn't necessarily require a fabulous singer. He chooses a very popular song from a recent Broadway hit that suits his voice perfectly. He's listened to the cast recording numerous times to help him prepare for this important audition. His friend has the song in a book of recent Broadway hits and has agreed to loan a copy of the song to Steve to take with him. He drops by her apartment to pick it up on his way to the audition.

He arrives and waits in the appropriate area. Shortly thereafter, his friend, Matt, arrives for the call. "Matt has never really studied voice," Steve thinks to himself, and he decides that he has a distinct advantage over Matt, since he's been working with a teacher for two years. Besides, this company will be glad to have someone who can really sing this role.

Steve's name is called. He enters the room at the appropriate time, presents his loose pages of music to the pianist, and takes center stage. After organizing the music and making some assumptions about tempo and style, the pianist begins the song.

Steve discovers right away that the piano accompaniment doesn't sound anything like the recording. He's not even sure where to make his first entrance in the music. The pianist cues him in. Once into the song, Steve finds himself struggling with the key, which is lower in pitch than the cast recording. The tempo is also slower than he wants it to be. Battling all this new information, he panics. He looks over to the pianist and starts snapping his fingers to the tempo he wants.

Now he's at the chorus of the song, and everything seems to be back on track until the pianist becomes confused. After shuffling the out-of-order pages, the pianist manages to find where he's supposed to be and continues.

Steve manages to make some beautiful sounds in spite of this disaster, sounds with which no one could possibly find fault. But in this key, the song doesn't show off his high note at the end because it's too low. The disappointment of the whole event registers on his face as he turns and leaves with his music. He can't figure out why the piano player couldn't play this popular song.

The casting committee, without a word, places Steve in the rejection pile. The casting director quips, "I'd give anything to see someone prepared to audition today. And how many more times are we going to have to hear that song?"

In the waiting area, Steve informs his friend Matt—and everyone else within earshot—how terrible the pianist is and how his audition was ruined by someone who obviously doesn't listen to cast recordings. Steve is out the door in a huff. Matt hears this news and figures that since he's not that great of a singer, he's doomed. After all, Steve has a great voice and chose a really great song. Matt has chosen an obscure song from a 1930s revue.

He enters the area nervously when he's called. Taking a deep breath, he approaches the pianist with his music displayed in a binder. Before taking center stage, he instructs the pianist as to how fast the song should be played by singing a few bars quietly. Because he's unsure in his singing, he also asks that his starting note be prominently played at the end of the introduction to the song, so he's certain to begin on the right pitch.

He takes center stage and the music begins. Sure enough, he gets the note and he's on his way. While the quality of his untrained voice isn't top-notch, his ability to sell the lyric is very strong. He understands that communicating the text must hap-

pen at all costs. Since he's rehearsed his song with a piano player several times already, he knows exactly how the song will
sound with accompaniment. Because there are little surprises for
him, he's able to concentrate on his goal: selling himself.

Once the song is completed, he thanks the committee and
the accompanist as he retrieves his music. A member of the committee asks Matt what show that song was from and indicates
that it's a nice choice.

After he leaves, the casting committee places Matt in the
callback pile, remarking that his acting ability, preparation, and
confidence were all very impressive. No one even discusses the
quality of his singing voice.

It's likely that neither Steve nor Matt will ever realize what
really happened here. Matt will probably tell Steve he doesn't
understand why Steve wasn't called back, and Steve is likely to
say that it's just luck and you never know what kind of pianist
you're going to get. Matt will be amazed that the pianist supported him while Steven will continue to wonder why the
pianist had it in for him.

Steve doesn't realize, however, that the pianist wasn't out
to get him, and that bad luck had absolutely nothing to do with
this disaster. With all the substandard auditions that pianists and
casting directors endure on any given day, you can bet that they
want to see people do well. Strong auditions are really rare.
Strong audition skills, even rarer.

What each of these men did right or wrong in the audition
has nothing to do with his singing abilities. Steve, first of all,
should have never chosen a song that is extremely popular.
Casting committees endure the latest hits hundreds of times a
day and are thirsty for something they haven't heard in a while.
Matt, however, chose a song that is not overdone, piquing the
interest of the committee. Steve made a few assumptions: that
the pianist would know the song and that he would play it exactly as it was done on the cast recording. Matt also made some
assumptions: that the pianist didn't know what he wanted and
that a tempo should be indicated. Steve, having picked up the
music just before the audition, had never rehearsed his song

with a pianist. Matt, being less cocky, took time to prepare and got a friend who played piano to help him. In the end, Matt got what he expected, and Steve got a lot of surprises.

Matt, unaware that his skills offer him a distinct advantage, doesn't realize that many people don't prepare the way he does. Steve will probably use the same song at least two more times before he decides it's cursed and must be discarded.

Having learned from Steve and Matt, let's look more closely at the dos and don'ts of auditioning—especially for an inexperienced singer.

Bring music with you to the audition. Never assume that a pianist will know your song and be able to play it for you in the right key. Don't laugh; it happens all the time. And don't be one of those people who has to sing "Happy Birthday" because there's no other alternative.

You should also present printed music in a binder, copied on two sides to eliminate the number of page turns (pianists are accustomed to turning pages). If you do this, don't use plastic covers for your pages. The glare from these can make the music difficult to read.

Another option is to tape the single-sided pages onto card stock side by side so they don't go plummeting to the floor. Many pianists prefer this to a binder. Regardless which method you use, loose-leaf pages will end up out of order or on the floor every time.

Choose an appropriate song. Appropriate songs are generally not from the latest Broadway musicals or national tours. Because songs from such shows are done so frequently, committees start to tune them out, no matter how well you sing them. For the same reason, avoid songs from musicals that are "household words" such as *Oklahoma, Carousel, Camelot, Guys and Dolls*, and *The Sound of Music*. Other inappropriate songs include those immortalized by Judy Garland, Frank Sinatra, or any other singer whose voice is immediately identified with them.

Most importantly, avoid "character" songs that require you

to play a specific role in a play. For example, you have to be playing the part of Eva Peron in order to sing "Don't Cry for Me Argentina." Likewise, avoid songs sung by characters not your age, type, or gender. Grown women should never sing "Tomorrow" from *Annie*, and songs that are narrative (tell some lengthy story) or instructive ("Put on a Happy Face" or "Make Someone Happy") belong in the shower, not on the stage.

So where do you find songs that are appropriate? As outlined in the previous chapter, look first at the music of Irving Berlin, Jerome Kern, and Richard Rodgers and Lorenz Hart. While some of their songs are overdone as well, there are some gems that work very well in an audition. Never assume that because you haven't heard the song before it hasn't been overdone. Ask around.

An appropriate song is one that enables you to be yourself, communicating a personal story or emotion. This presents you as a three-dimensional person. Let the committee members make decisions about which roles you're suited for—they will anyway.

Rehearse your song with a pianist. The scenario described at the beginning of this chapter clearly demonstrates the need for this. There will be enough surprises in performing your song with the audition accompanist as it is. Don't risk it further by going in without a clue. In the process of rehearsing the song, you will discover if it's in the right key for you. If it's too high or too low, then you must find it in an appropriate key, have it transposed professionally, or discard it.

Never ask the audition pianist to transpose your song. Even if he's willing to do it, you run the risk of huge mistakes. Besides, bad audition form negates any success you have. If you ask someone to transpose it for you in advance, have it printed from a computer program or make sure the handwritten manuscript is legible. When transposing, make sure the lyrics and vocal line are written in as well. The pianist can get lost if he doesn't know where you are in the song at all times. After you get the transposed copy, take it to a pianist and rehearse it to check for clarity and errors.

Present yourself as a singer. Never apologize for your singing voice, no matter how weak you may think it is. Allow the casting director to decide what you have to offer. Many actors apologize by their own lack of confidence, playing mind games like "Since I'm not that great, I should let you know I'm not that great so you don't think I'm stupid." Don't waste your time with apologetic behavior. Just sing.

Communicate the song at all costs. Choose a song that says something about you and share it. Remember: an actor who relies on his acting ability while singing is much more likely to win the role.

Say "thank you" when you're finished. There's never an inappropriate time to be polite. After the song is over, wait a beat, then say, "Thank you." This lets the committee members know that you're finished. It also opens up the opportunity for them to ask for more information.

These guidelines, if followed carefully, will make even the most inexperienced singer passable at a call. Start by changing your audition habits and see what kind of results you get. If nothing else, you'll feel better about the experience, knowing that you went in prepared and confident.

In the meantime, find a qualified teacher and continue to develop your skills as a singer. There are great singers out there with great audition skills who win the part every time. Don't be one of those who can't compete because you don't know the rules.

This chapter doesn't begin to cover the many aspects of auditioning. I encourage you to pursue further study of the audition process as your singing skills develop. Take a look at *How to Audition for the Musical Theatre* by Donald Oliver (Portsmouth, NH: Smith & Kraus, 1985); *Next! Auditioning for the Musical Theatre* by Steven M. Alper (Portsmouth, NH: Heinemann, 1996); and *On Singing Onstage* by David Craig (New York: Applause, 1991). These books are invaluable to a singing actor.

Afterword

If you take nothing else from this book, let it be these words: "Success comes in cans, not in cannots." If you believe that you have the ability to sing, then you are a singer. If you have a voice with which to say, "I'm not a singer," you have contradicted yourself with your own singing instrument.

Imagine a new, well-tuned guitar string that of its own volition refuses to play. Like this string, which is designed to vibrate and create a beautiful tone, you as a human being are designed to sing. You cannot choose or disown something you were born with.

It may sound like an infomercial, but I see it happen all the time: someone discovers a voice he or she didn't know was there. I am told that in assisting that discovery I've done something amazing, something a student could never have done on his or her own. This is only true to a point. The work I do is simply a matter of helping someone unlock a door. The actor must be willing to make the journey of his own accord.

So put aside such problematic labels as "actors who sing" and "singers who act." This is a challenge for all performers who want to express themselves—and gain employment—in one of the century's great art forms, the musical theatre. Who knows? As with any extracurricular challenge that seems to be peripheral to your "real" acting goals, whether it's charity work or learning a foreign language or traveling the world, you might find that singing informs and inspires you to new heights on stage. At the very least, you'll learn something about yourself—a topic every actor can afford to know more about.

Exercise your right to sing.

Kevin Robison can be reached online at theactorsings@yahoo.com. *He welcomes your questions, comments, and personal success stories.*

Suggested Reading

Finding Your Voice: A Spiritual Guide to Singing and Living, Carolyn Sloan (New York: Hyperion, 1999)   Sloan offers a refreshing, positive process for discovering a voice that is honest, truthful, and uniquely yours. Includes exercises in vocal technique as well as important student examples.

Freeing the Natural Voice, Kristin Linklater (New York: Drama Publishers, 1976)   The definitive discussion of the speaking voice for the actor, offering the most thorough process for releasing unhealthy vocal habits and discovering the natural resonance of your voice.

On Singing Onstage, David Craig (New York: Applause, 1991)   With his engaging wit, David Craig offers an important series of exercises that enable the actor to communicate a song truthfully and honestly, especially in an audition situation.

The Diagnosis and Correction of Vocal Faults, James McKinney (Nashville: Genovox, 1994)   In spite of its unfortunate title, this book offers an in-depth study of the singing voice, outlining common habits that impede the technical and performing processes.